GOD'S
SUPERNATURAL
POWER
IN YOU

ANOTHER BOOK BY FRANK DeCENSO

Amazed by the Power of God

AVAILABLE FROM DESTINY IMAGE PUBLISHERS

GOD'S
SUPERNATURAL
POWER
IN YOU

Frank DeCenso Jr.

DESTINY IMAGE® PUBLISHERS, INC.
P.O. Box 310, Shippensburg, PA 17257-0310

*"Speaking to the Purposes of God for This Generation
and for the Generations to Come."*

This book and all other Destiny Image, Revival Press, Mercy Place, Fresh Bread, Destiny Image Fiction, and Treasure House books are available at Christian bookstores and distributors worldwide.

For a U.S. bookstore nearest you, call 1-800-722-6774.
For more information on foreign distributors, call 717-532-3040.
Or reach us on the Internet: www.destinyimage.com.

ISBN 10: 0-7684-2832-7
ISBN 13: 978-0-7684-2832-2

For Worldwide Distribution, Printed in the U.S.A.

1 2 3 4 5 6 7 8 9 10 11 / 13 12 11 10 09

CONTENTS

INTRODUCTION

And He Himself gave some to be apostles, some prophets, some evangelists, and some pastors and teachers (Ephesians 4:11).

THE PASTORS AND TEACHERS AND MINISTERS who have contributed to this collection of chapters (as well as to the chapters in Volume One, *Amazed by the Power of God*) have done so to educate and equip the Church to walk in God's Kingdom power today. In this introduction, I would like to express my God-given motive for compiling such a collection of chapters about how to move in the power of God today.

A Christian Leader's Job Description

When you think of a pastor, prophet, or teacher, do you have clear ideas about their purpose? Maybe you think that a pastor is to effectively govern a church body and feed inspiring messages to the flock. Perhaps a prophet's role in today's Church is a bit more confusing for you to understand—you may even question the validity of the need for prophets today. A teacher's role isn't so hard for you to imagine; they should teach the Bible and spiritual truths, right?

Ephesians 4:11 leaves us no choice but to accept the reality that the ministers Paul mentioned have been given to the Church for a reason, and nothing in Scripture indicates an expiration of their necessity within the Church. We should thus conclude that there are apostles, prophets, evangelists, pastors, and teachers today, even if we aren't quite clear on their roles. Paul, however, leaves no ambiguity about their primary function in the building of Jesus' Church:

> *...for the equipping of the saints for the work of ministry, for the edifying of the body of Christ* (Ephesians 4:12).

Those in Christian leadership—apostles, prophets, evangelists, pastors, and teachers—have a specific assignment from Jesus. That assignment, which is given in Ephesians 4, doesn't entail making believers feel good about themselves, become better people, or cognitively learn wonderful truths. The assignment is to equip the members of the Body of Christ to become workers in *ministry*.

Unfortunately, many in leadership do not equip believers to do works of ministry. Instead, they focus on building robots who seek self-help techniques. Or they strive to sound like wise and wonderful shepherds of spiritual truth who can lead their flocks to pastures where the spiritual buffet is a 24/7 feast of new and exotic spiritual food.

Clearly that is not what Jesus called leaders to do. Leaders are to equip, equip, and then equip some more. The question of this introduction is: who is equipping believers to minister to the sick, dying, demonized, hurting, brokenhearted, and homeless, and to the rest of humanity?

Equipped or Stripped?

Unfortunately, observation leads me to conclude that believers are not being equipped; they're being stripped—stripped of the purpose that develops from being trained as Jesus trained His disciples. This training is needed for believers to become "power-from-on-high" ambassadors of God's Kingdom who can partner with Jesus in ministry to reach the people of this world.

This equipping and training ultimately comes from a believer spending intimate time with Jesus and garnering His insight on how to minister effectively.

> *But He said to them, "Let us go into the next towns, that I may preach there also, because for this purpose I have come forth." And He was preaching in their synagogues throughout all Galilee, and casting out demons* (Mark 1:38-39).

Notice that Jesus said, *"Let us go."* He wanted His disciples with Him as He preached and demonstrated the Gospel by casting out evil spirits. He did not take them to show off His preaching abilities and power. Rather, He took them to model Kingdom ministry—preaching the Kingdom of God with demonstrations of the Kingdom He preached about.

Later, Jesus sent His disciples out *on their own* to do the same ministry of preaching and power.

> *Then He appointed twelve, that they might be with Him and that He might send them out to preach, and to have power to heal sicknesses and to cast out demons* (Mark 3:14-15).

> *And as you go, preach, saying, "The kingdom of heaven is at hand." Heal the sick, cleanse the lepers, raise the dead, cast out demons. Freely you have received, freely give* (Matthew 10:7-8).

Just as Jesus took His disciples with Him, trained them to minister with demonstrations of power, and then sent them out, so also He wants to equip and send us out. One way that we are equipped to do His works is by spending time with Him *before and as* He sends us out. This process is circular and continuous. Jesus gave us the Holy Spirit to be with us and to accompany us on every ministry journey.

He'll teach us before, during, and after we step out in His power to minister to the inhabitants of earth.

The apostles also used this model of training and equipping.

And Barnabas and Saul returned from Jerusalem when they had fulfilled their ministry, and they also took with them John whose surname was Mark (Acts 12:25).

It is possible that Mark was taken along for training purposes since we see him shortly after called an assistant (see Acts 13:5). Later he assisted Barnabas:

...And so Barnabas took Mark and sailed to Cyprus; but Paul chose Silas and departed, being commended by the brethren to the grace of God. And he went through Syria and Cilicia, strengthening the churches (Acts 15:39-41).

Silas is described as a prophet earlier in the text (see Acts 15:32), so Paul took someone who already had ministry experience. But Barnabas took Mark as his assistant, and I believe it was for Mark's continued equipping. Much later, Paul asked that Mark would visit him, implying that Mark had been well trained by Barnabas.

Only Luke is with me. Get Mark and bring him with you, for he is useful to me for ministry (2 Timothy 4:11).

Barnabas mentored Mark into a place of maturity where Paul believed him effectively equipped for ministry.

Where Have the Mentors Gone?

Where are the mentors today? Are leaders taking congregants and followers alongside to show them how to minister and then releasing them into ministry? Perhaps in some places it is happening, and for that, I thank God. But I believe some leaders are afraid that equipping believers for ministry will make those under their leadership feel like they actually have to *work* for the Kingdom. The false notions that Christianity is supposed to be a joy ride to the pearly gates and that the leaders should do the ministry since (in many cases) they are paid by the church are being perpetuated, perhaps unknowingly, by mistaken models of leadership.

The Great Commission, as it's been termed, is a call to make disciples, not just student converts.

> *"Go therefore and make disciples of all the nations, baptizing them in the name of the Father and of the Son and of the Holy Spirit, teaching them to observe all things that I have commanded you; and lo, I am with you always, even to the end of the age." Amen* (Matthew 28:19-20).

A biblical disciple is someone who lives and acts as taught and equipped by a mentor. To make disciples, we have to be willing to spend time with new believers, ensuring that they are fully equipped to meet the demands of the same Commission that brought us into the Kingdom of God.

Jesus said that discipling should happen through *"teaching* [believers] *to observe all things that* [He]...*commanded* [the disciples]*"* (Matt. 28:20). The "all things" that Jesus referred to here must include those things that He told His disciples to *do* during their ministry journeys. On many occasions, Jesus commanded the disciples to go to various locations, preaching and also demonstrating the Kingdom through miraculous works. Jesus didn't tell the disciples to only teach new believers the great wisdom that He had spoken about to them. So we can reasonably conclude that the discipleship Jesus referred to includes both the teaching of truth as well as the equipping for Kingdom works.

Today's discipleship methodologies must include demonstrations of and hands-on training in Kingdom works. Just as Jesus and the early Church demonstrated the presence and power of God's Kingdom, today all believers must be equipped to do the same Kingdom works which includes healing the sick, raising the dead, delivering the demonized, freeing those in bondage, and performing other activities that visibly demonstrate the Kingdom of God.

Following are some passages that illustrate what Kingdom ministry looks like:

*Truly, truly, I say to you, he who believes in Me, the works that I do, he will do also; and greater **works** than these he will do; because I go to the Father* (John 14:12 NASB).

And as you go, preach, saying, "The kingdom of heaven is at hand." Heal the sick, cleanse the lepers, raise the dead, cast out demons. Freely you have received, freely give (Matthew 10:7-8).

But He said to them, "Let us go into the next towns, that I may preach there also, because for this purpose I have come forth." And He was preaching in their synagogues throughout all Galilee, and casting out demons (Mark 1:38-39).

Then He appointed twelve, that they might be with Him and that He might send them out to preach, and to have power to heal sicknesses and to cast out demons (Mark 3:14-15).

Then He called His twelve disciples together and gave them power and authority over all demons, and to cure diseases. He sent them to preach the kingdom of God and to heal the sick (Luke 9:1-2).

But when the multitudes knew it, they followed Him; and He received them and spoke to them about the kingdom of God, and healed those who had need of healing (Luke 9:11).

And heal the sick there, and say to them, "The kingdom of God has come near to you" (Luke 10:9).

Now, Lord, consider their threats and enable Your servants to speak Your word with great boldness. Stretch out Your hand to heal and perform miraculous signs and wonders through the name of Your holy servant Jesus (Acts 4:29-30 NIV).

And through the hands of the apostles many signs and wonders were done among the people. And they were all with one accord in Solomon's Porch (Acts 5:12).

And believers were increasingly added to the Lord, multitudes of both men and women, so that they brought the sick out into the streets and laid them on beds and couches, that at least the shadow of Peter passing by might fall on some of them. Also a multitude gathered from the surrounding cities to Jerusalem, bringing sick people and those who were tormented by unclean spirits, and they were all healed (Acts 5:14-16).

And Stephen, full of faith and power, did great wonders and signs among the people (Acts 6:8).

And the multitudes with one accord heeded the things spoken by Philip, hearing and seeing the miracles which he did. For unclean spirits, crying with a loud voice, came out of many who were possessed; and many who were paralyzed and lame were healed. And there was great joy in that city (Acts 8:6-8).

Now it came to pass, as Peter went through all parts of the country, that he also came down to the saints who dwelt in Lydda. There he found a certain man named Aeneas, who had been bedridden eight years and was paralyzed. And Peter said to him, "Aeneas, Jesus the Christ heals you. Arise and make your bed." Then he arose immediately. So all who dwelt at Lydda and Sharon saw him and turned to the Lord (Acts 9:32-35).

Therefore they stayed there a long time, speaking boldly in the Lord, who was bearing witness to the word of His grace, granting signs and wonders to be done by their hands (Acts 14:3).

Now God worked unusual miracles by the hands of Paul, so that even handkerchiefs or aprons were brought from his body to the sick, and the diseases left them and the evil spirits went out of them (Acts 19:11-12).

Jesus wants to build a Church that is completely active in Kingdom ministry. When He walked the earth, He took 12 flawed humans along for a three-year course on how to minister with power in order to change lives. Today's leaders need to disciple their followers in the same manner, teaching them that all believers are called as Kingdom ministers and sending them out to reach the world.

How can this world be touched by God's powerful love if the Church just warms the pews and listens to wonderful sermons? Let us not strip the Church of its purpose—a purpose birthed by being equipped to do the works of Jesus.

If we want a vibrant, spiritually mature Church, we must minister according to Jesus' pattern: *everyone* must be equipped and released to minister.

From whom the whole body, joined and knit together by what every joint supplies, according to the effective working by which every part does its share, causes growth of the body for the edifying of itself in love (Ephesians 4:16).

My prayer is that this book will challenge leaders and believers alike to equip and to be equipped.

Chapter 1

WARRIOR'S MANTLE

Dr. James W. Goll

I DID NOT HAVE ANY CHOICE about being born, and neither did you. However, I did have a choice about being *reborn*, and so did you. You and I made the choice, though, without realizing that we were about to be reborn into a war zone. When we signed the dotted line and volunteered freely for the day of His power, nobody told us (until later) that we were born in a war and that we were born for war. Yes, you enlisted into the army of God!

Now we find ourselves in the middle of a conflict between two warring kingdoms: the kingdoms of light and darkness. We are in a spiritual war of historic proportions. The war between these two kingdoms had been going on for a long time, before any of us arrived, and it is still raging. In fact, we have entered the drama toward the end of the last act, when it all heats up.

You and I have come to the realization that, although the outcome of this war has been predetermined by Jesus' death and resurrection, we enlisted in an end-time struggle of good and evil, right and wrong, righteousness and darkness, till the very end. We cannot get out of it. We are on active duty, day in and day out.

The book of Numbers mentions that there is a Book of Wars, which has never been discovered by any earthly archeologists (see Num. 21:14). Maybe that is because there is a heavenly Book of Wars in which some war stories are still being written—and some victory songs are yet to be sung. You and I may find out some day that some of our battles were recorded in that great, triumphant read.

But in the meantime, we are engaged in the actual warfare. And even though we did not volunteer knowingly for this, we do have the ability to determine how we will fight and what weapons we will use. We have both the power to fight and the delegated authority to win. We can choose to put on our warrior's mantle. In fact, we must learn to stand and fight with the power of His might and to enforce the victory of Calvary.

The Fame of His Name

It's all about Jesus. Jesus Christ has given us His Holy Spirit so that we will have the supernatural clout of the Son of God. All true spiritual warfare is ultimately centered on the placement of the Son of God in our lives, our families, our cities, and our nations. Jesus is to be high and lifted up, and all of the worship goes to and through Him to God our Father. That is how the warfare began before Lucifer's fall (see Isaiah 14:12-15; Ezek. 28:12-19: Luke 10:18-20; Rev. 12:4,12), and that is the basis upon which it continues. All true spiritual warfare centers on the placement of the Son! After all, this is about the fame of His great name being spread throughout the earth.

Jesus is the Son of God who sits upon His throne at the right hand of God the Father Almighty. In the beginning, there was no warfare. But lucifer (later referred to as satan) couldn't stand to see

16

God getting all of the glory. His jealousy, competition, envy, and divided loyalty shattered the unity of Heaven. You know the story.

Now, having allied ourselves with the Father, we find ourselves in the middle of a battle against satan's demonic forces of darkness. Those evil forces are temporary, to be sure, but they are very, very determined to take out as many as possible before the end.

Your battle is not against your spouse, your children, or your boss. It is not against your pastor or the person who won the last election. Your struggle is against unseen enemies:

> *For our struggle is not against flesh and blood, but against the rulers, against the powers, against the world forces of this darkness, against the spiritual forces of wickedness in the heavenly places* (Ephesians 6:12 NASB).

The fact that you struggle does not mean that you have done something wrong. (I am assuming that you are on the right side!) Struggle is actually a sign of life and proof that you have not been conquered. We must struggle to come through on the other side.

Your Job Description

I have a job description for you from the Bible: destroy the works of the devil. "*...The Son of God appeared for this purpose, to destroy the works of the devil*" (1 John 3:8 NASB). We have the same job description as He does since everyone who belongs to the Son of God is supposed to be like Him. "*...And the Lord—who is the Spirit—makes us more and more like Him as we are changed into His glorious image*" (2 Cor. 3:18 NLT).

Those are your marching orders: destroy the works of the devil. Put satan under your feet. Crush the head of the enemy. *"The God of peace will soon crush Satan under your feet..."* (Rom. 16:20 NASB).

When you put the devil under your feet, Jesus puts him under His feet. The battle in which we find ourselves is a battle to the finish. In the end, everything and everybody will be under His feet:

Therefore God also has highly exalted Him and given Him the name which is above every name, that at the name of Jesus every knee should bow, of those in heaven, and of those on earth, and of those under the earth (Philippians 2:9-10).

Your Warrior's Mantle

Each of us has a different role to play in this battle, but in order to fight, we have to put on the warrior's mantle. You have read about the armor of God in Ephesians 6:13: *"Therefore, take up the full armor of God, so that you will be able to resist in the evil day, and having done everything, to stand firm"* (Eph. 6:13 NASB).

Now it is time to recognize that, beside your armor of God, you also have a warrior's mantle, which you wear over your armor. Just like the armor of God, this mantle is spiritual and supernatural. But the fact that you cannot see it with your eyes and feel the rough fabric does not mean that it's not just as real as the shirt that you put on this morning.

Your warrior's mantle signifies your authority in Christ. It also signals your selection by God, and it indicates a level of anointing that corresponds to your level of authority.

When Elijah wanted to call Elisha to follow him, he cast his mantle onto Elisha's shoulders (see 1 Kings 19:19). But for most of us, no Elijah will ever come and do that. We need to be more like Elisha at the end of Elijah's life, when he *persisted* in following his master Elijah doggedly until he obtained a double measure of Elijah's anointing by obtaining his mantle (see 2 Kings 2).

Over Here Right Now!

Because the battle is long, we need to exercise that kind of persistence repeatedly. One time, I was hungry and desperate to have my warrior's mantle renewed. I had been doing too many meetings in a row without receiving anything myself. I ended up at a big Rodney Howard-Browne meeting in St. Louis, Missouri, with two good friends of mine.

We were just attending the meeting, not leading it or speaking at it. I was so desperate and hungry for more of God. I normally led meetings and rarely got to attend gatherings for my own spiritual input. My friends, who are real men of God, were acting a bit more reserved than I was. They are both brilliant men who deeply love Jesus, and they too wanted more from the Lord. They were sitting next to me as my hunger within began to arise.

Across the auditorium, Rodney Howard-Browne, revivalist from South Africa, was ministering. He had a microphone, and he was looking across the crowd and slowly praying for people the way he often does. He would lay his hands upon people and say, "Fill!" People were responding and being filled and overwhelmed with the presence and power of God. I couldn't stand it any longer.

Right then, I saw something that I wanted. I saw the power of the Holy Spirit in raw form. I just wanted more of God. Browne didn't seem to be in too much of a hurry as he worked his way among those at the front of the large auditorium, praying, "Fill, Fill, Fill." He was like the King of Slow that day. I wanted him to come over to my side of the sanctuary. So I began to raise my voice and relentlessly say, "Over here! Over here right now!"

My two distinguished friends were now slinking down into their chairs, possibly a bit shocked at my "blind Bartimaes" cry. They knew Jim Goll as the dignified prophet—not the wild man who would do anything for more of the Lord. I just kept hollering, "Over here! Over here right now!"

Finally, Rodney Howard-Browne came to our side of the auditorium and started up the aisle. He reached out his hand and touched me in the midst of my desperate cry. When he touched me, I slouched and froze in a 45-degree angle position for about 20 minutes. I fell into a trance (which is in the Bible; remember Peter in Acts 10), and I was caught up in the Spirit, where the Lord imparted more of His presence, purpose, and power to me. While I was in that state, the Lord asked me a question. He said, "When you first got baptized in the Holy Spirit, what happened to you?"

I could barely think, but I answered, "The first thing that happened is that You, Jesus, became more real to me."

Then the Lord said, "The second thing that happened was that the enemy became more real too, and he tried to steal away from you and others what I had just given." After that, He downloaded to me all sorts of ideas for books, study guides, training materials, and the like. He commissioned me to begin to supply His people with what they would need in order to be prepared for the next move of God. He commissioned me to release transferable concepts to ground people in the word of God so that the enemy would not be able to kill, steal, or destroy the Holy Spirit's authentic impartations.

Casting Off the Cloak

What really happened that day? God clothed me with a fresh warrior's mantle. But first I had to cast off my old garment, which was a garment of desire for a good reputation. I had to throw it to the wind. Honestly, I wore dignity with a man-pleasing manner. I had to get so desperate that I did not care what people thought of me as I shouted, "Over here!"

In those days, one of my goals—and it seemed like a good one to me—was to give some dignity and respectability to the prophetic movement. I wanted to present good, solid teaching, and I wanted to have a good reputation. That was a nice goal, a dignified goal. But I had to leave it behind at that Rodney Howard-Browne meeting in order to press on in God.

I had to be like blind Bartimaeus:

Then they came to Jericho and as He was leaving Jericho with His disciples and a large crowd, a blind beggar named Barti-maeus, the son of Timaeus, was sitting by the road. When he heard that it was Jesus the Nazarene, he began to cry out and say, "Jesus, Son of David, have mercy on me!" Many were sternly telling him to be quiet, but he kept crying out all the more, "Son of David, have mercy on me!"

And Jesus stopped and said, "Call him here." So they called the blind man, saying to him, "Take courage, stand up! He is calling for you."

Throwing aside his cloak, he jumped up and came to Jesus.

And answering him, Jesus said, "What do you want Me to do for you?" And the blind man said to Him, "Rabboni, I want to regain my sight!"

And Jesus said to him, "Go; your faith has made you well." Immediately he regained his sight and began following Him on the road (Mark 10:46-52 NASB).

Just as blind Bartimaeus had to throw off his cloak of false security in order to run to Jesus, so we need to throw something old off before we can be clothed with new strength. Our time of desperation is prime time for the Spirit of God to renew our strength and to clothe us with a warrior's mantle.

Your warrior's mantle will deliver you from the spirit of intimidation. It's a chicken-and-egg thing, though. Which comes first?—throwing off the spirit of intimidation in order to be clothed with the warrior's mantle or being clothed with the warrior's mantle so that you can overcome the spirit of intimidation? Whichever way it works, I know it is important to cast off certain things before we are in the position to receive the new ones.

I remember so well when, in that same season, the Lord visited my dear wife, Michal Ann, for nine straight weeks. Angels came night after night and the manifested presence of God increased day after day. And there was great fruit. A devoted woman of God was set free from the debilitating spirit of fear, and then, clothed in her own warrior's garment, she was used to set thousands free.

Faith Always Fights

It takes a certain amount of tenacity to fight in this battle. You cannot be a pacifist. Faith always fights: *"From the days of John the Baptist until now the kingdom of heaven suffers violence, and violent men take it by force"* (Matt. 11:12 NASB).

The battle has highs and lows. It ebbs and flows, but the enemy never ceases his assaults against the purposes and people of God. It seems that fiercer battles always tend to precede the advancement of new beginnings and new spiritual levels.

Through every challenge, we shall pursue our strong enemy *until*. There is always an *until*. Sometimes we get a revelation, and sometimes there is a manifestation, but always there is an in-between time, an *until*. But persevere we must! Fight until!

"I pursued my enemies and overtook them and I did not turn back until they were consumed" (Ps. 18:37 NASB). I pursued my strong enemies *until* I overcame them. From the days of John the Baptist *until* now, the Kingdom has been a violent struggle, and it is the forceful, persistent ones, the ones who never give up, who will win in the end.

You never know how long you will have to struggle or how long you will have to wait for the *until* of your promise to change into a *fulfill*. Just keep fighting. See your *until* clause through. Each day of battle makes your waiting time one day shorter—from promise revealed to promise fulfilled.

The amazing thing about a great boxer is that he rolls with the punches and never quits. Though I have taken heavy hits, I am determined to never, never, never quit.

The "D" Tactics

We need to be tenacious and determined because the enemy of our souls will do everything he can to defeat us. He cannot often succeed in taking one of us out of the battle completely, but he will always try to delay, deceive, distract, and disappoint us. In fact, delay, deceit, distraction, and disappointment are four of his favorite tactics.

But God can turn those tactics inside out and use them to make you stronger. When the enemy takes a swing at you, what do you do? Often, you become just a little desperate. OK—you become very desperate. Are you ready to be desperate for God? Will you pursue your strong enemy? I have been, and I am yet to this day.

You must be willing to release your hold on your old "cloak of security" long enough to receive a new warrior's mantle. Delay, deceit, distraction, and disappointment, when turned to the Lord, can even be used to make you more desperate and determined to keep pursuing God as Elisha pursued Elijah. Are you in pursuit of the anointing, or have you stopped along the way?

Why does the enemy attempt to attack you? Let me give you a few ideas. The enemy is jealous of the attention that you receive from the Lord of Hosts. You are the potential source of the pleasure of God. God not only loves you—He takes pleasure in you. The enemy cannot stand this. Have you considered that you are a threat to the enemy? Yes, you are a threat to the kingdom of darkness. The Anointed One lives inside of you, and you are close to His heart. The enemy aims his attacks at those who are closest to the heart of God—just ask a Jewish person. The enemy hates those who are close to the heart of God! But you must press in to the Lord because greater is He who is in you than the one who is in the world (see 1 John 4:4).

The enemy despises breakthroughs. Satan and his league of demons also attempt to prevent the arrival of supernatural assistance from the Lord. The devil wants to paralyze your planning, abort your dreams, and dilute your hope. He opposes anything that will give God glory. So let's put delay, deception, distraction, and disappointment under our feet in Jesus name. Pursue your strong enemy *until*.

Your Most Effective Weapons

Stick with your highest weapons. Here are a few weapons that you need in your arsenal in order to be an overcomer:

- You must know and speak the Word of God (see Rev. 12:11; Heb. 4:12; 1 John 5:4-5).

- Your conversations should reflect the mentality of a conqueror (see Prov. 18:21).

- You must take authority over satan and his demonic forces in the name of Jesus (see Prov. 18:10; Phil. 2:9-10).

- You must, by faith, clothe yourself with God's spiritual armor (see Eph. 6:13).

- You must tap into the power of prayer and fasting (see Isa. 58:6).

- You must draw forth the wisdom of God from spiritual veterans (see Prov. 1:5).

- You must maintain a life of praise to the Lord (see 1 Sam. 16:23; Ps. 149).

- You must learn when to rest and not directly engage the enemy (see Dan. 7:25; Hebrews).

- You must keep your testimony fresh and declare that God is good all of the time (see Rom. 10:8; Prov. 18:21).

- You must learn to come into agreement with God's word, will, and ways (see Matt. 18:18-19).

- You must sow seed in your time of need (see Mal. 3:10-11; 2 Cor. 9:6-12).

- You must declare what the blood of Jesus has accomplished for you (see Heb. 10:23; 12:22-24; Rev. 12:11).

Never Give Up

I am never going to quit; how about you? I know the Overcomer. You do too. We know who the Victor is, and He "mantles" us with His own courage, strength, wisdom, and everything else that we will ever need.

I am filled with Jesus, the Victor. I was born in war, and I was born for war. I am a weapon of spiritual warfare, and I get to enforce the victory of Calvary. I get to speak the very words of God: *"All Scripture is God-breathed and is useful for teaching, rebuking, correcting and training in righteousness"* (2 Tim. 3:16 NIV). I get to rebuke the devil. I get to speak the Word and watch the enemy flee. The Word is useful for teaching and correcting and training in righteousness—but also for rebuking!

Are you with me in this fight? Stand up, cast off your old cloak, put on your warrior's mantle, and let's get going. Be clothed with a warrior's mantle, and always remember, all of the time, to give God all of the glory.

NOTES AND APPLICATIONS

Chapter 2

FOUNDATIONS OF POWER MINISTRY

Dr. Che Ahn with Bessie Watson Rhoades

Now Is the Time

NOTHING IS MORE EXCITING than participating in this move of God that is sweeping the earth. God is releasing signs, wonders, miracles, and healings. The reaper is overtaking the sower (see Amos 9:13) as multitudes are being ushered into the Kingdom. The final preparation of the Bride is at hand—and God is using more than a select few people to do it!

He is using "the saints" in power ministry. As my respected friend, Dr. Bill Hamon, says in his book by the same title, this is *The Day of the Saints*.[1] Quite simply, we are going where the Church has never been before. It has taken two thousand years to get here. Now we are beginning to understand that *all* of us have the same Holy Spirit and that we are *all* invited to walk in the authority and image of Jesus.

As we look back, we see that God has incrementally restored to His Bride many key truths, such as the knowledge of salvation by grace, the gift of tongues and the infilling of the Holy Spirit, and the truth about and need for the fivefold offices. We have now come to a time in history when the power and glory of God underscore

His work and revelation through us. No longer is "power ministry" and the miraculous an occasional testimony; it is becoming a way of life for the believer.

Birthed by receiving God's grace through intimacy with Him, the miraculous is available to anyone who seeks it with a pure heart and faith. We are leaving behind the old "celebrity" model of ministry and walking into the truth that God always intended to have a powerful Church. When He established the fivefold ministry, He commissioned apostles, prophets, evangelists, pastors, and teachers to *"equip the saints for the work of the ministry"* (Eph. 4:11-12). We have spent too many years with *only* the fivefold ministers *doing all* of the work! No wonder ministers quit! A few can't do the job of millions!

A Matchless Privilege

While there are many definitions of power ministry, my focus is on that which is birthed only through supernatural capability and demonstration. I'm not talking about spiritual gifts, pulpit ministry, teaching, discipling, or prayer. Nor is my focus on outreach or even large crusades, although all of these are of God and require the Holy Spirit to be successful.

I'm focusing now on what I consider to be power ministry: remarkable miracles, unusual signs and wonders, exponential salvation, and visible demonstrations of the power of the Holy Spirit, such as healing.

I also believe that power ministry includes revelational expressions, such as visions, dreams, interpretations of dreams, words of knowledge, and prophecy. Finally, I define power ministry as observable manifestations of the glory and presence of God through the Holy Spirit in supernatural operation. Examples of this include being "slain in the spirit" (falling over under the presence of the anointing) and other supernatural physical manifestations, such as when the apostle Paul was knocked to the ground by God (see Acts 9:4), when Peter walked on water (see Matt. 14:29), and when Jesus walked through a solid wall or door (see John 20:19).

To me, the purpose of each of these manifestations is not to appear impressive to those present, but to glorify Christ by leading individuals into revelation, faith, and transformation. The ultimate goal is the transformation of cities and nations. Power ministry is a demonstration of Heaven's *normal* mode of operation released on earth *now* by those who believe that the Kingdom is *at hand*— which literally means "within our grasp" (see Matt. 10:7).

Not of Ourselves

I know better than anyone that it is not within my power to open blind eyes, to cause cancers to shrink and disappear, to see thousands saved in a day, or to speak a word of knowledge that forever changes a human heart.

And yet God has chosen me as a conduit, and I willingly say "Yes!" What impresses me is not that He chose me or even the degree of power and authority that He allows to pass through my life. Instead, it is the privilege of seeing people delivered of oppression, healed of heart-wrenching illness, saved from hell, restored in relationships, and loosed to live a life that brings Jesus glory.

He has provided the sacrifice of His Son, the grace of the Holy Spirit, and even my desire to step into this place of ministry. None of it is of my own doing.

When I look into the eyes of a person who has received a miracle or been set free, I know that I am seeing what Jesus saw when He talked about the *"joy that was set before Him"* (Heb. 12:2). It is the inexpressible gratitude and awe in that person that gave Jesus the ability to endure the cross. While I have never experienced the degree of pain that He bore, I forever thank Him for His sacrifice. His death not only gave us salvation, but it also gave each of us the same privilege and grace of walking in supernatural ministry that sets others free.

Your Character

As I asked the Lord what I could best share in this compendium, I felt it was not as much of what the Lord has done *through* me, but rather what He has done *to* me to allow me to function and be established in power ministry.

It's one thing to start a fire or light an explosive; it's another thing to keep it burning and effective in the long run. I feel the same way about power ministry. It's not just the miracles that interest God—but the man or woman who is representing His name. It is not just the "big bang" of a healing or an unusual sign that impresses Jesus; it is the character of a person that will sustain His glory and bring honor to His name.

Many of us have to learn these lessons the hard way. While we need not falsely minimize who we are in Christ or our authority as believers, our emphasis must always be on Jesus and not on us. The most obvious challenge is to not be impressed with ourselves because He allows us to use *His* power! This even happened to the apostle Paul. He went from considering himself equal with the twelve apostles to finally recognizing himself as the chief of all sinners (see 2 Cor. 11:5; 1 Tim 1:15). Somewhere between these two books of the Bible, he must have had a revelation.

I am sure that, on more than one occasion, God has had a good laugh at those of us who misunderstand our use of someone else's tools when we present ourselves as the manufacturer. I have found that the more God uses me in power, the more humble I become. I am simply discovering that *"…it is no longer I who live, but Christ who lives in me…"* (Gal. 2:20). It's Jesus alone who's "doing the stuff" and allowing me to partner with Him.

What Interests God

As revival approaches, many more believers will begin to flow in power ministry. The prophets in the land have been declaring for several years that we are in a time of acceleration. Not only are more people getting saved in a shorter amount of time, but personal growth in individuals and in the Church is also accelerating. In this season, knowing and heeding the foundational truths of character and ministry are more important than ever.

How do you build your life wisely in order to facilitate power ministry? The cost for one who wants to move in signs, wonders, and power is higher than for those who choose to simply be saved and sit in the background. A person "hiding out" until He comes is really no threat to satan and the forces of hell. But those who step into power ministry may easily become "front line" victors or (sadly) casualties, depending on the foundation they lay.

For which of you, intending to build a tower, does not sit down first and count the cost, whether he has enough to finish it—lest, after he has laid the foundation, and is not able to finish, all who see it begin to mock him, saying "This man began to build and was not able to finish" (Luke 14:28-30).

God loves risk-takers and overcomers, and He is pleased only by those who walk in faith (see Heb. 11:6). In fact, the Bible says that He takes no pleasure in those who *"shrink back"* (Heb. 10:38 NASB).

But He also has laid out strategies for us to keep us running the race in such a way so as to win (see 1 Cor. 9:24). You need to count the cost daily and follow His plan in order to finish well.

Begin With the Basics

Early in my walk, the Lord impressed on me the importance of the basics, of prayer and obedience. Both are extremely vital, yet easy to forget.

As John Wesley said, "God does nothing on earth save in answer to believing prayer."[2] Jesus called His Church a house of prayer (see Matt. 21:13). He was consistently praying, seeking the Father's will, rising early to spend time with His Father, and telling His disciples that He did nothing of His own accord, but only what He saw the Father doing (see John 5:19). To only do what you see the Father doing requires that you spend enough time *with God* to know what He is about! Too often, we rush off to do our own thing and simply ask God to bless it on the way. That is not how God intended us to operate.

Nothing has changed since Jesus followed His Father's lead— so it should be the same for you and me today. Prayer gives us the Father's heart and priorities, and it also changes ours. In fact, perhaps the most important part of prayer is that it changes *our* minds, not God's. We become like Him as we connect with Him (see 1 John 3:2). In that manner, we display His intentions and not our own.

Prayer should *be* our lifestyle. Paul encourages us to pray without ceasing (see 1 Thess. 5:17). An effective way to do this is to pray in tongues. Praying in tongues builds you up and assures pure communication with the Father. It gives you strength for the task at hand and often redirects you when you would have chosen to do something differently. We may plan our way, but the *"Lord directs our steps"* (Prov. 16:9).

We all too often decide what "makes sense" to us and rush off to do it without consulting the Lord. We are never so mature that we do not need to pray about what to do and how to do it.

Even King David, wise in matters of war, constantly asked before each battle, *"Shall I go up"* (1 Sam. 23:2). Even when he had won a mighty campaign just a few days earlier, he did not put confidence in what worked yesterday in order to determine what was right for today.

God made manna to spoil if it was used more than one day (see Exod. 16:20). The same applies to yesterday's "portion" from the Lord. We need to seek our new portion each day and let the Lord direct our steps. We often need to stop in the middle of an activity (even public ministry) and pray to see if the Spirit has shifted or is redirecting us to a different method, a time of silence, a time of prophecy, etc., so as to stay attuned sharply to His will.

Continually seeking His face in prayer is not a work of the flesh or something to put on a "to do list." The grace to pray is a gift in itself and part of an intimate relationship with God. I believe it comes by being continually filled with the spirit, as proscribed in Ephesians 5:18. We need to be filled anew every day in order to operate in the supernatural. It is this same filling that keeps us from walking in the flesh. As we daily walk in the Spirit, we grow in the sanctification and holiness that reflect God's character in our lives (see Gal. 5:22-23).

Yet prayer can be virtually ineffective if we are not *obedient* to what God is showing us through it. It may be obedience to how long we spend in His presence or how we care for our family or others in our ministry. It may be obedience in taking care of ourselves or in financial discipline. It may be the small obedience of hearing His voice and responding quickly to His prompting, even if it seems odd or unnecessary. While it may not seem relevant to moving into the realm of power ministry, we must be willing to be obedient in the small or unpleasant areas of our lives. Otherwise, what confidence can God have in us that we will follow Him in bigger and often more crucial instruction? (See Luke 16:10.)

I have found that, in my personal journey toward seeing blind eyes healed, if God asked me to pray for someone with a headache or a hangnail, my refusal to do so would hinder the fulfillment of greater works in the future.

Likewise, if I am out running around looking for someone to pray for at the mall when the Lord has asked me to be home spending time with my family, I have also missed the mark. Though an activity may look good, if it is self-initiated, it is still disobedience.

If God asks you to pick up a piece of trash, take home a person who needs a ride, or give $10 to a stranger, you must obey with the knowledge that these actions are just as "spiritual" as the "big" prayers. God's prompting alone determines the importance of your actions. And He is not impressed when you choose which of His commands you will obey based upon their importance in your eyes.

I have a friend who the Lord once prompted, at a stoplight, to follow the car in front of her and to pray for the driver. She thought it odd and came up with a myriad of excuses for why, as a single woman late at night, this would not be sensible. She actually refused to do it, passing the car as it turned into a mini-mart. As she drove past, the Lord told her, in the voice she had heard so many times before, "If you would just be obedient, something very important will happen." She turned around and went back to the market.

The time was 11:45 P.M. The driver turned out to be an older woman desperately seeking an answer from God. She cried as my friend delivered the word. The woman then told my friend that she was planning to take her own life after midnight if she received no reply from God. We never know in advance why our obedience is so critical, but God does. We are wise to obey.

Faithful With Little

When counting the cost of walking in power ministry, where do you place the importance of keeping your check book accurate, paying the rent on time, giving back what isn't yours, and tithing? Do you think these little duties might be irrelevant when it comes to seeing the lame walk?

It is not so in God's eyes. Luke 16:10 tells us that, if you are faithful with little, you will also be faithful with much. Moreover, Jesus states, *"Therefore, if you have not been faithful in the unrighteous mammon, who will commit to your trust the true riches"* (Luke 16:11). Surely the true riches are spiritual gifts and the intimate knowledge of God. These are priceless to the believer. Yet they are reserved for the one who has been found faithful in little. God is interested in the one who has paid what he owes and considers honesty and integrity in small things just as important as in big things.

The very next verse says, *"If you have not been faithful in what is another man's, who will give you what is your own"* (Luke 16:12). I believe this applies to how reliable you are with things that belong to others—especially in ministries that you may be serving. Perhaps it is another's offering that you are counting, their building that you are cleaning, or a small group that you are stewarding. Do you treat it as your own and take great care?

How you serve others will likely be how others will serve you. Your faithfulness and trustworthiness in daily activities helps determine how well you will handle the choicest of spiritual riches.

You may have heard that what you do in secret shows who you really are. Nothing about us is hidden from our Father, so we would be wise to give a righteous accounting in all that we do. We can find no shortcuts to character. If an area in your life needs special attention, humble yourself and seek healing or restoration so that it will not cause your failure in the future.

Although you may think that God is taking too long to release you to your heart's desire, you must know that He is investing carefully in your life in order to undergird the coming power so that it won't destroy you or others in the process.

If you had a son who showed little responsibility in most areas of his life, would it be wise for you to buy him a turbocharged vehicle at 16 that could cost him his life? Or would it make more sense to help him buy a reliable car until he proves himself able to handle greater responsibility? The Lord, as a Father, has the same prudent affection for us. He cares deeply about our character.

Thus, instead of focusing on the big ministry that we don't yet have, we must focus on the foundation of all ministry—our character. We need to follow through on integrity in large and small things, including resolving conflicts, making phone calls that we'd rather avoid, reading the Word when we don't feel like it, and choosing to honor our relationships and spend time with our families or spouses when we had something else in mind.

A Level and Balanced Life

Sadly, if we read about many of the spiritual greats who moved in historic power ministry—such as William Branham, or many others who fell—we discover the tragedies that they encountered in their personal lives in the form of alcohol or prescription addiction, failed relationships, the love of money, sexual immorality, false doctrine, and more. Most of their failures were rooted in the pressure to carry the anointing without having true accountability or receiving assistance from others.

We are blessed to find ourselves in a time when the fivefold ministry is being re-established and most church movements are implementing godly structures and apostolic alignment to oversee their ministers and to offer help when needed. This is to our benefit. I would never think of moving alone in the dimension of power ministry that the Lord has bestowed upon me without the blessing of other godly leaders. I want godly men and women speaking into my life and giving guidance as needed. I believe that mutual submission to peers and those more mature in the Lord is an absolute necessity and that team ministry and the counsel of others is wise.

I pray you will make these tenants vital priorities as well. Even as He sent out the early apostles two by two, God is revealing that team ministry is a safeguard in many ways. First, it is a very practical means to prevent burn-out and exhaustion. It is also a great deterrent from satan's traps of temptation and from the assaults of the enemy. Two have exponential power when it comes to spiritual opposition—one puts a thousand to flight; two put ten thousand to flight (see Deut. 32:30).

In the "thrill of the moment," while moving in power ministry, watching blind eyes become clear, a person cast off a leg brace, or a thousand rush forward for salvation, we often forget that we are running a marathon, not a sprint. We are in this for the long haul, while we have breath or until Jesus comes.

That is why balance is such an important facet of our lives. I personally care about you as I write this because I know firsthand the problems that ensue when our priorities are out of alignment with God's best.

These include personal priorities, such as taking care of your body (exercise, proper rest, and nutrition) and guarding your family life. Many ministers wrongly sacrifice their families or their children "for the sake of the Gospel" when this brings shame to the name of our Savior.

My family intentionally sets aside time to nurture our relationships in the midst of busy schedules. For example, after 29 years of marriage, I still "date" my wife on a weekly basis. We also have a family dinner on a weekly basis, even though two of my children are married. Thank God that they live close by and are active at Harvest Rock Church, where I pastor.

At all times, we are *"living epistles to be read of all men"* (2 Cor. 3:2). Are you living in such a way that anyone would want to convert to what you represent?

The other type of balance is ministry balance. If we are just doing series of "glory" or "miracle" meetings, we must ask ourselves when the infrastructure is being built into the lives of those participating. We are to make disciples, not spectators or receivers. We must teach others the foundations of the faith and the importance of giving away what they receive. *"Freely you received, freely give"* (Matt. 10:7-8).

We need to be connected with and lead others to resources and training centers and churches as we move in power ministry so that "lasting fruit" can be grown in those who are touched, healed, or saved.

Another important balance is reproduction. The objective is not a few "sainted ones" who are capable of walking in power ministry. Rather, our goal is for all of God's people to walk in the revelation that they *are* sons and daughters of God (see 1 John 3:1). It means embracing the truth that we are made in *His* image and are given *all* of His inheritance. As Jesus said to His Father, *"For I have given them the words which you have given Me..."* (John 17:8). He went on to pray, *"The glory which You gave Me I have given them..."* (John 17:22). We need to *believe* and *act* on the mandate, *"Greater works than these* [**you**] *will do"* (John 14:12). What an awesome promise!

God is waiting for a Bride with whom He can be *equally* yoked, and that necessitates that we walk in some pretty impressive power!

Discerning Good and Evil

It is amazing to me how many aspiring ministers are not well-versed in the Word.

Certainly, this is a cause for Bible Schools, but I believe that knowing God's Word is a non-negotiable for every believer. We must set our focus on the Word to study and apply it all the days of our lives. The Word alone is our ultimate umpire on the truth of what is set before us. We will need that standard often.

Moving on to the "meat" of the Word is especially important. *"Solid food belongs to those who are of full age, that is, those who by reason of use have their senses exercised to discern both good and evil"* (Heb. 5:14).

The Word trains us to walk in power ministry in many ways. First, the Word is a record of testimony. Such testimony builds our faith that we too can operate in this dimension. We can see how miracles happened, when they happened, and who God chose.

Second, in the Word we can see the growth of a minister's life. David did not take on Goliath as his first conquest, but he had already overcome the lion and the bear (see 1 Sam. 17:34-36). In the same way, many are not prepared to pray for a cancerous tumor during their first ministry trip; we start with what is set before us and learn to grow and discern.

Growth in discernment is one of the most important aspects of ministry. God has given us senses. When consecrated and not given over to ruling our spirit, our senses serve as keen guidance in following the Lord's lead.

This is especially true in the revelational and prophetic gifts, such as word of knowledge, prophecy, and word of wisdom. When we have our senses trained, we grow in discerning what the Lord is saying. He may speak to you by pulling on your heart out of compassion for a certain individual (He did this with Jesus in Mark 1:40ff). Or He may speak to your spirit. You may find that certain verses jump out of the Word, giving guidance or insight to your immediate situation. You may receive pictures or visions in your mind while awake or dreams while asleep. Most people experience "butterflies," or an inner knowing, when they are receiving a truth or information that God wants them to release.

As you release these words (and in the process, discover if they are of the Lord), your confidence will grow, and your level of accuracy and reception will increase. Don't be afraid to fail as you share what you receive. Just offer your insights in humility because you are learning and growing in these gifts. No one is right all of the time. The Word says, *"We know in part, we prophesy in part"* (1 Cor. 13:9). We do grow!

The Word provides us with wonderfully powerful gifts. When we read the Bible as our record of testimony, we learn that Jesus' one word of knowledge to the woman at the well brought an entire town to salvation (see John 4:1-42). That is power ministry!

Elisha and his servant's vision of the unseen forces of God gave his servant faith that they would win the battle when they were greatly outnumbered (see 2 Kings 6:8-23). It was pretty important that Ananias received a word of knowledge regarding where to find Saul (Paul) to pray for his sight to be restored, thereby winning one of the greatest leaders of all Christendom (see Acts 9:10-19). Receiving this kind of information from the Spirit takes practice. It is the same for words of knowledge about healing—both inner healing and physical healing. Having such a word greatly increases the receiver's faith for a miracle or life change.

As you grow in discernment, it will affect every aspect of your ministry. You will know better how to hear the Lord on where to go and on when and where to meet certain people.

Jesus, as always, is our example. His seemingly untimely decision to wait two days before going to pray for Lazarus brought forth power ministry to a whole town (see John 11). Another time, Jesus released power ministry by putting the unbelievers out of the house before he prayed to raise a little girl from the dead (Mark 5:40).

Of course, as in any training, there is trial and error. My friend, Heidi Baker, whose ministry in Mozambique has seen more than 30 dead people raised and thousands of others healed of deafness, blindness, and more, tells how she prayed for the first 99 people with no results. The 100th was healed instantly. Another friend, Stacey Campbell, received numerous prophetic words that God was going to use her in a major healing ministry. For more than 10 years, little happened when she prayed. But she kept praying. And now she is consistently walking in signs, miracles, and wonders—and she's glad she didn't give up!

Practical Growth

In addition to reading the Bible as a training manual for operating in power ministry, you should also read accounts of the lives of those who have operated in it. Learn and dream with God about your desires for the miraculous, and discover how others have moved into it successfully.

You might also sit under the teaching of ministries that model what you desire to do. Learn from their style, format, and results. This doesn't necessarily mean that you have to change churches or move to a different city. In this media age, you may be able to simply sign up to receive their weekly teaching or watch their services on video streaming or television.

Another wise choice would be to attend some of the new "power ministry" schools. These programs cost less and are shorter than conventional Bible schools, and they focus more on teaching and training in the use of the power gifts. They prepare you in a shorter time to put your dream to work on the mission field, in your downtown area, or in your neighborhood, school, or workplace.

Attend every good conference that you can on the supernatural and those that offer impartation of the power gifts. Buy the CDs or DVDs if you are not able to go. You would pay for and attend a university course on a subject that you needed to learn, and this mode of learning is cheaper and easier to use.

Take every opportunity to minister, and ask regularly for feedback and correction. Try a home group before you jump into the pulpit. Do you love healing and miracles? My friend Bill Johnson says we should consider those with crutches, casts, and wheelchairs as "fair game." Hardly anyone will turn you down if you sincerely and politely ask if you can pray for them.

Go to nursing homes, homeless shelters, and jails to put your gifts to work. Hone the skills that make your initial approach successful so that you don't turn people off before they can see Jesus in you.

Grow up in your level of faith by simply exercising your gifts and obedience. If possible, join a mentor program or request mentoring from those who currently minister in your areas of interest so that you can be more personally trained.

Make use of the power of the testimony. Read as many books as you can about miracles and power ministries, including biographies of the great revivalists. These works will fuel your faith and your passion. You will also find that they will build your confidence that you too can do the greater works that Jesus referred to (see John 14:12).

Always Remember...

In our quest for ministry that delights God and surely delights us, we must never forget the apostle Paul's greatest pursuit: *"That I may know Him, and the power of His resurrection, and the fellowship of His sufferings..."* (Phil. 3:10).

Our intimacy with the Lord is our greatest purpose and delight. From that place, everything else that is meaningful or lasting flows. You will move in power ministry when you are intimate with God. That's His *modus operandi.* As we partner with Him, we will see individuals, cities, and even nations transformed for His soon return. Come, Lord Jesus!

Endnotes

1. Dr. Bill Hamon, *The Day of the Saints* (Shippensburg, PA: Destiny Image Publishers, 2005).

2. John Wesley, quoted in Dutch Sheets, *Intercessory Prayer* (Ventura, CA: Gospel Light, 1996), 23.

Notes and Applications

Chapter 3

THE SECRET IS THE SECRET PLACE

Dr. Heidi Baker with Shara Pradhan

The Secret to Revival

Therefore, my brethren, you also have become dead to the law through the body of the Christ, that you may be married to another—to Him who was raised from the dead, that we should bear fruit to God (Romans 7:4).

PEOPLE OFTEN ASK, "What is the secret to revival?" The secret place is the secret to revival. In the midst of my busy life overseeing thousands of churches, caring for thousands of children, and feeding thousands of people every day, Jesus spoke to me to reverse my schedule. He wants our time. He said, "I want you to come away, my beloved. I want to woo you. I want to love you. I want you to live in this secret place. If you give me your mornings, I will give you a nation."

Holy Passion

My commissioning to the nations started by being called as His Bride. Many years ago, Jesus came to me in a vision. A bright white light surrounded me, and I heard the external, audible voice of God for the first time in my life. I was 16 years old. Jesus said that I was to be married to Him. Oil ran down my arm, and I felt Him kiss my left ring finger. He said, "You are called to be a minister and a missionary. You are called to Africa, Asia, and England." When the presence of God lifted, I was alone in the church. I had been still with my hands raised for nearly three hours. Incredible joy hit me, and I began to preach the next day. I have been preaching and living a life of missions ever since. God called me to give my life for the poor.

My husband, Rolland, and I have been missionaries for 28 years in Asia, Europe, and Africa. Since that divine commissioning, I have preached the Gospel. And still the Lord speaks to me to simplify. Still the Lord says that He wants more of my time. He asks me for my mornings. I live in the holy chaos of overseeing Iris Ministries and caring for so many children in our beloved Village of Joy in Pemba, Mozambique. And at times, I hear God saying, "Come away, my beloved and walk on the beach; come and ride your bike with me; come and lay down in my presence." And my little religious heart is thumping as I get overwhelmed by the ever-present needs.

One of my life passages is John 15, which is about abiding in Jesus, remaining in the vine so that our lives can bear much fruit. I know that God, as the master vine dresser, wants to prune and chop away things that are religious to draw us into the secret place of His heart. Revival is impossible outside of divine union and communion with Him. He is not as concerned with how much we can do for Him as with how much holy passion fills our hearts for Him. Lovers outwork workers. There is nothing I would not gladly give my King. And God responds, "In that case, I want your time."

Living Under Water

And it shall be that *every living thing that moves, wherever the rivers go, will live. There will be a very great multitude of fish,*

*because these waters go there; for they will be healed, and
everything will live wherever the river goes. It shall be that fish-
ermen will stand by it from En Gedi to En Eglaim; they will be*
places *for spreading their nets. Their fish will be of the same
kinds as the fish of the Great Sea, exceedingly many. But its
swamps and marshes will not be healed; they will be given over
to salt. Along the bank of the river, on this side and that, will grow
all kinds of trees used for food; their leaves will not wither, and
their fruit will not fail. They will bear fruit every month,
because their water flows from the sanctuary. Their fruit will be
for food, and their leaves for medicine* (Ezekiel 47:9-12).

I live to spend time with Him. I live to be fully possessed by
His glorious presence. God yearns to draw us so deeply into this
Ezekiel 47 river that we do bear fruit all 12 months of the year, that
our lives do bring healing to the nations, that we go beyond ankle,
knee, or waist deep; we go until we are fully immersed in the ocean
of His liquid love. Only from this place of full possession can we
truly be used by Him.

I take this passage in the book of Ezekiel quite literally! When
God told me that He wanted more of my time, I rearranged my
daily schedule in Mozambique so that I do not start before 11 in
the morning, except for times of prayer. I love to wake up really
early to the African sunrise and spend hours with my Jesus. The
more people press in with needs and crises, the more I must press
into His presence. The greater the daily challenges, the more I must
pray. Every day, I must seek His face and worship Him.

Sometimes I stick on a snorkel and swim out in the turquoise,
tropical, clear Indian Ocean. I swim out away from the never-ending
cues, lists of demands, and ever-present crises. Deep, deep in the
water, I am finally alone with Him. I love swimming into that silent
underwater garden where I am away from everyone else, and I can

hear His still small whisper. I worship under water and admire His beautiful creation. I delight in being alone with Him—just Jesus, me, and often a bright yellow little fish. An hour may pass by as I simply pray, "Lord Jesus Christ, beautiful Son of God, have mercy on me, your beloved." Some might look upon this and think that I am being lazy. Some might even think I am irresponsible to go snorkeling or riding my bike when there are still hungry people to be fed, churches to oversee, and children to care for. But the more I have to do, the more I must press into prayer. I have no choice but to be utterly dependent on Him.

I have to live in the secret place of His heart. In Pemba, every week we see villages run to Jesus. Since the Lord spoke to me five years ago to move to Cabo Delgado, in order to get His lost Makua bride, we are seeing village after village love Him. The Makua tribe was the most unreached people group in southeast Africa, according to missiologists. Since Jesus sent our ragtag Iris family of missionaries and Mozambicans to Pemba, we have seen hundreds and hundreds of churches planted among this tribe. Most weeks, Jesus opens up deaf ears as He is opening the ears of our nation to hear the good news of the Gospel of Jesus Christ. Each day, He miraculously provides food for the hungry. Each day, I watch His Kingdom break forth with His glorious light in spite of challenges too great to tell. Weekly, we have crises and problems which would make your heart faint. But He brings peace in the storms. And in the midst of it, we see Jesus.

Yet even as we see revival break forth, Jesus told me that His favorite time of my day is the mornings. He loves it when I snorkel or ride my bike or simply lay down in a quiet place with my heart fixed on Him. I love to pray in that underwater garden. I love to pray while looking at His beauty. It is just me adoring Him. I do not pray through a list of intercessory needs, though that is a good thing to do. I do not tell Him how to feed the people, because He knows how to feed them.

I want to know nothing but Christ and Christ crucified (see 1 Cor. 2:2). I just swim or ride or rest and love Him: "Holy, holy, holy. Worthy, worthy, worthy. I love you! I love you!" And He spoke to me, "Heidi, this morning time is my favorite time of our day." He loves our intimacy more than miracles, more than seeing villages saved, and even more than seeing orphans fed. Like Romans 7:4 teaches, in order for us to bear fruit to God, we must be intimate with Jesus. All fruitfulness flows from that place of laid-down love. All fruitfulness flows from intimacy.

God longs to be loved. He wants to know that He is more important than revival. He must be more of a priority than the multitudes, than the fruit, than the miracles. When we are that in love with Him, fruit happens. It is effortless in love.

I have one goal and that is to be such an intimate lover of Jesus that I am a resting place for the Holy Spirit. I want to be so one with Him that I become like Him, love like Him, and radiate His very nature until I become a resting place for His presence. More happens in one single minute in the anointing than in a lifetime of labor and efforts. We can do nothing by our own efforts. It is not by might, not by power, but only by His spirit (see Zech. 4:6).

We can do nothing apart from His presence. Like my morning snorkel swim or bike ride, our entire ministry must flow from His Holy Spirit. There is a place in the Spirit where you can cast out the Ezekiel 47 nets when you live inside the very heart of Jesus. Only then can you spread out nets so that Jesus can catch fish from every tribe and tongue. Only then can we be like those fruit trees which bring fruit all year long. Only then can our lives truly bring healing to the nations.

The water in this passage flows from the sanctuary. Likewise, our whole lives must flow from the holy of holies. God does not want a worship service but unceasing union and communion. We must give never-ending adoration to our King Jesus. When we live from this place of being fully submerged in the ocean of His liquid love, we will bear fruit to bring healing to the nations. There is a place of supernatural fruitfulness where our lives are so deep in His glory that exponential fruit pops out of each one of our little laid down lives of love.

If you are not in love, you should quit.

First Commandment First

The first step in ministry is to be intimate with Jesus. Our greatest joy in life is to be married to Jesus so that we can give our lives away without fear, just as He did for us. My goal, even in this chapter, is that you would fall so deeply in love that there would be no "no" left in you when responding to the high calling of God. When you are so full of the presence of God, when a person meets you, they meet Him. When you hold them, Jesus holds them. Then Jesus becomes irresistible to them.

Missions, ministry, and revival are defined by laid-down passion at the foot of the cross. There we pray, "Possess me, Holy Spirit, that I might be conformed into Your image. Let me reflect the majesty of who You are."

Love God and Your Neighbor

My mission statement for Iris Ministries for nearly three decades is simple: love God, love our neighbor. This is the five-year plan. This is the 10-year plan. This is the 20-year everything message.

Love God with all your heart, mind, soul, and spirit, and love your neighbor as yourself (see Luke 10:27). Be one with each other and one with Christ Jesus. To make this possible, Jesus died and rose from the dead.

What is God's goal? He wants every single person in this world to know Him. He wants every man, woman, and child to be taken in as His sons and daughters. He wants His house to be full.

He made Heaven big enough for everyone. Because He died, there is always enough. How can the Gospel go forth to the ends of the earth so that none should perish? Paul the apostle answered this very question by writing, *"fulfill my joy by being like-minded, having the same love, being of one accord, of one mind"* (Phil. 2:2). This is the reason why we give up our homes, our families, our possessions. It is not so that we will look like we are doing something good. We give everything to God as we follow the Lamb who was slain. He gave everything to us. We choose our lover. We choose to be married to Him. If we choose Him, then in Him, we have all that we need.

A New Breed of Ministers

Missions is not about where you are; it is about where He is.

Love knows no limits, places, or bounds.

Revival starts with seeking His face.

A new breed of ministers is rising up; they will not wear out for the Gospel. They are so caught up in passion, union, unity, and fullness that they will run out and say, "Congo, here I come!" And if they get shot at, they are thrilled. And if they don't get shot at, they are thrilled. If the place is filthy, they are thrilled. If it is clean, they are thrilled (see Phil. 4:11-12). He is the joy set before them (see Heb. 12:2). He is their exceedingly great reward. Their lives are full of joy unspeakable and full of glory (see 1 Pet. 1:8).

The secret of revival is the secret place. Missions is not about where you go; it is about where He is. He has to move on the inside of you. You have to feel His heart before you will have anything to offer anyone else. Then, when you have rested your very head against His chest, like John the beloved, you can move according to His heartbeat.

Despite traveling hundreds of thousands of kilometers last year, I find myself at home wherever I am. And I find myself at home everywhere I go. When I am in Korea, I love Korea! When I am in Brazil, I am Brazilian! Of course, Mozambique is my favorite place on earth. It is truly home. When I know that God sent me somewhere, I am happy there. I live for Him. It is all about this passion; it is all about where He is. The most important things for me are union with Him and embracing the one in front of me.

Joy in the Holy Spirit

For the kingdom of God is not eating and drinking, but righteousness and peace and joy in the Holy Spirit (Romans 14:17).

Ministers should be the most joyful, in-love people on the planet. The Gospel is not a competition in misery. I remember living in Asia where missionaries seemed to compete to see who could be the most miserable. Many would boast in their newsletters about how difficult it was suffering for the Gospel. From their perspective, the one who suffered the most would surely get brownie points in Heaven for misery. I have been shot at five times, I have been beaten and thrown in jail, and I have fasted often. I know a bit about suffering and pain. And yet, I count it as nothing. I count it as joy (see James 1:2). If you want to export misery, then find another profession. Joy is contagious. If we are not full of Him, we have nothing to offer anyone else.

Unstoppable in Love

Ministry ought to be the most contagious, outrageous, Holy Spirit adventure this side of Heaven.

In October 2005, I almost died in the hospital from a MRSA infection. I determined that I would not die in that way! I would not die of a dirty, flesh-eating disease. I want to be a martyr for Jesus one day.

However, it is easy to die for Jesus, and it is more difficult to live fully for Him. I do not want to just die well; I want to live well. Until my last breath, I want to give everything that I am for all that He is. As Mother Teresa wrote, "You love until there is pain; you love through the pain until all that remains is love."

If you are really in love, then it is a joy to suffer for the Gospel. If you feel pain, get deeper and closer to His heart. Press in for the face-to-face presence. Nothing will seem difficult when He is only a breath away.

The amount of crises that we deal with at Iris in any one day is ridiculous. If we were not in love, we would be in a mental institute! But we are not in a mental institute because we are in love. When crises come to me and press in on me, one after another, I just have to look into the eyes of the One I love. He is always enough!

I want to be fully possessed by His Holy Spirit until I am completely overshadowed by God. I want to be utterly overtaken. My prayer is that we would all stay hidden inside of God's glorious heart of love until we are manifesting His nature as sons and daughters, living, breathing, moving, healing, and giving life to others just as Jesus did. My prayer is that we would not even pursue power, but His presence, that we would not only seek revival, but also His face, that we would determine to live in the secret place of His heart.

The Fire of His Eyes

Set me as a seal upon your heart, as a seal upon your arm; for love is as strong as death, jealousy as cruel as the grave; its flames are flames of fire, a most vehement flame. Many waters cannot quench love, nor can the floods drown it... (Song of Solomon 8:6-7).

Many do not know how to live in the secret place. Many do not understand intimacy. Beloved, it is simpler than we think. It is just about letting Him love us.

Every time I have had a vision or impression of Jesus, I have always been undone by His eyes of love. They are like liquid flames of fiery love. Many waters cannot quench this love. Focus on His face, Church. Focus on His heart, Bride. If we have the courage to lock gazes with Him, He can purify our hearts. When He looks into us with His eyes like a flame of fire, eternity is branded on our hearts.

We must behold His face to become like Him. Then we can dwell in the fire of His embrace. Isaiah 33:14-15 reads, *"...Who among us shall dwell with the devouring fire? Who among us shall dwell with everlasting burnings? He who walks righteously...."* To dwell in this fire, we must fix our eyes on Jesus. Then, when people peer into our eyes, Jesus will look back at them.

I believe God wants to pour out fresh salve to give us His eyes to see and His ears to hear a lost and dying world. We have made our God too small; we imagine that He has limits. When we do not have His eyes, we start to see God in our image rather than seeing humanity in the image of God. We must have pure eyes to see God for who He is. When we see God for who He truly is, we will want to be pure. And we will know that He is big enough for all of our needs. You cannot meet all of your needs because you are not God. God is God, and we are not!

When we see with God's perspective, it is so much bigger than our own. Recently I had another visitation. I was picked up by two angels, one on each side, and we began to fly across the nations of the earth. The angels handed me golden oil as I saw multitudes of sick, dying, and broken people. I flew with the angels over nations and poured this liquid, golden oil like honey upon the people. They all fell on their faces. Everyone was healed. I saw this huge, incredible harvest like nothing I had ever seen before. I am now beginning to experience this harvest and the fulfillment of that vision. His heart is big enough to love the entire world.

Again, the secret to revival is the secret place. The secret to fruitfulness is intimacy. We must remain in God if God is to remain in us. It is impossible to bear fruit outside of life in the vine. In a time when He is shaking everything that can be shaken (see Hag. 2:6-7) and ministers and ministries are being tested and pruned, we must finish well in Him.

God wants more time with us. The only way to run the race well is to look at Jesus. When we fix our gaze only on Him, all things are possible. God is looking today not only for powerful people, but for intimate lovers who are so overshadowed with His presence that His glory may hover over them.

The more time we spend with God, the more fruitfulness will happen in our lives. Our ministries will be greater than what we have ever dreamed of. We must not look at our inability but gaze into the eyes of the Only Able One. We are never able on our own. It is all about Him. He is able. So let Him draw you past the outer courts into the Holy of Holies. Go so deep, past the knees, past the waist, until you are in over your head.

Final Prayer: Abide in Him

Let Him love you. It is so much simpler than we thought. It is time to be transformed by His love so that there is no fear in you. Be wrecked for everything but His presence. Be so utterly and abandoned in His love.

God in His glory will pour His presence into people to the degree that entire nations will be transformed. He will pour His love out like a river, like an ocean. Let Him kiss you with the kisses of His mouth. Dive into His heart.

It's time to lie down and let God be God. He is mighty, and nothing is impossible with Him. He wants to kiss His church, and transform you with His love. We are called to be carriers of His glory. It is not about being an eloquent speaker, man of power for the hour, or great revivalist. It is about being so close to the heart of God that you know what He's thinking. Then you are not afraid to go anywhere and say anything as His radical lovers. He captivates us so that we can never go back. He wants to shatter your box. Often our God is still too small. It is time for whole nations.

Lie down so that He can trust you with everyone. Then when you get up there is revival—when whole nations come to Him, falling on their faces. He changes us with one glance of His eyes, so that we are not afraid to be completely abandoned in His arms. Many want lots of power and anointing, but when we just lie down and let Him love us to death and kiss us back to life, it is a truly powerful thing.

He is looking for union, not occasional worship so that our very nature is transformed. We must walk in His nature, and we must die daily.

Again all fruitfulness flows from intimacy. To the degree that we are untied with the heart of Jesus, God will bring fruit in our lives. To the degree that we are in love with Him, we will be fruitful. We cannot make revival happen. But we can become so hungry for God, we become a prisoner of love. And these prisoners of love, these harvesters, will so carry His glorious presence, the hungry can no longer resist anymore.

I am the true vine, and My Father is the vinedresser. Every branch in Me that does not bear fruit He takes away; and every branch that bears fruit He prunes, that it may bear more fruit. You are already clean because of the word which I have spoken to you. Abide in Me, and I in you. As the branch cannot bear fruit of itself, unless it abides in the vine, neither can you, unless you abide in Me. I am the vine, you are the branches. He who abides in Me, and I in him, bears much fruit; for without Me you can do nothing. If anyone does not abide in Me, he is cast out as a branch and is withered; and they gather them and throw them into the fire, and they are burned. If you abide in Me, and My words abide in you, you will ask what you desire, and it shall be done for you. By this My Father is glorified, that you bear much fruit; so you will be My disciples. As the Father loved Me, I also have loved you; abide in My love. If you keep My commandments, you will abide in My love, just as I have kept My Father's commandments and abide in His love. These things I have spoken to you, that My joy may remain in you, and that your joy may be full. This is My commandment, that you love one another as I have loved you. Greater love has no one than this, than to lay down one's life for his friends. You are My friends if you do whatever I command you. No longer do I call you servants, for a servant does not know what his master is doing; but I have called you friends, for all things that I heard from My Father I have made known to you. You did not choose Me, but I chose you and appointed you that you should go and bear fruit, and that your fruit should remain, that whatever you ask the Father in My name He may give you (John 15:1-16).

NOTES AND APPLICATIONS

Chapter 4

Divine Healing Power[1]

Jaeson Ma

Then He called His twelve disciples together and gave them power and authority over all demons, and to cure diseases. He sent them to preach the kingdom of God and to heal the sick.... "Whatever city you enter...heal the sick there, and say to them, 'The kingdom of God has come near to you'" (Luke 9:1-2; 10:8-9).

Therefore go and make disciples of all nations, baptizing them in the name of the Father and of the Son and of the Holy Spirit, **and teaching them to obey everything I have commanded you...** (Matthew 28:19-20 NIV).

Go into all the world and preach the gospel to every creature. He who believes and is baptized will be saved; but he who does not believe will be condemned. And these signs will follow those who believe: In My name they will cast out demons; they will speak with new tongues; they will take up serpents; and if they drink anything deadly, it will by no means hurt them; **they will lay hands on the sick, and they will recover** (Mark 16:15-18).

In March of 2006, an intercessor friend of mine walked up to me and said, "Jaeson, I've been meaning to share with you this dream I've had for a few months. In this dream I saw you standing in the middle of a university with crutches in your hands. Empty wheelchairs and stretchers were all around you. Then I saw Smith Wigglesworth, the great healing evangelist, walk up to you and offer you his mantle. But this mantle wasn't just for you; it was a mantle for all the students you work with on different college, university, and even high school campuses, to release the power of divine healing to this generation."

After he shared this dream with me, I was shocked, because just the day before I had pulled out my 500-page Smith Wigglesworth autobiography to read. I had asked God in prayer, "Lord, would You stretch out Your mighty right hand and release the healing anointing of Smith Wigglesworth over the campuses of America once again!" Wigglesworth was one of the greatest healing evangelists and preachers in history. He raised more than a dozen people from the dead and had faith like no other.[2] When praying for the sick he would preach, "Fear looks, faith jumps! Only believe," and, "I am not moved by what I see. I am only moved by what I believe."[3] I knew this prophetic dream of Smith Wigglesworth was timely—a confirmation and prophetic sign that the Holy Spirit is releasing His healing power, right now, to this generation.

It was only a few weeks later that the outbreaks of divine healing occurred at UCLA on Bruin Walk. The fraternity brother miraculously started walking without his crutches in front of the crowd of on-looking students after we prayed for him. Many were weeping at the sight of it; the healing presence of God was so strong and the power of God was present for all to witness. The people were in awe of God's power and I knew it was a confirmation of the prophetic dream I had received weeks before.

Indeed, this is just the beginning. In the coming days we will see supernatural healings occur on our campuses night and day with regularity. What happens when the star basketball player gets his broken arm healed instantaneously because you prayed for him and news got out? What happens when the miracle-working power of Jesus breaks out so strongly in the middle of campus that students are being healed of sicknesses and infirmities daily in the campus courtyards? What happens when word catches wind, the entire student body comes to watch, the gospel is preached and hundreds, even thousands are saved? Why not? It happened when Jesus walked the streets of Galilee; it happened in the book of Acts, when entire cities were shaken by the disciples (see Acts 19:1-20); it will happen again today. We owe this generation an encounter with God. It's not enough to talk a good theology; it's time to demonstrate God's power. It will happen when we become compassionate for souls and passionate for divine healing.

The Power of Divine Healing to Save the Lost

Scripture tells us:

Then Jesus went about all the cities and villages, teaching in their synagogues, preaching the gospel of the kingdom, and healing every sickness and every disease among the people. But when He saw the multitudes, He was moved with compassion for them, because they were weary and scattered, like sheep having no shepherd (Matthew 9:35-36).

The word *compassion*, in the Greek, is *splanchnizomai*,[4] and it means to be moved with deep compassion or pity.[5] It was Jesus' compassion and deep love for people that motivated Him to heal the sick. He saw them as "weary," or as another translation says, "harassed and helpless." Scholars believe this word can also be translated "pinned-down and molested."[6] Jesus was so hurt, so moved, so pained at the lost state of Jerusalem that it was like

67

watching the devil pin down and molest God's children. He could not take it. His compassion moved Him to action. I pray that we too are moved with compassion when we walk the streets of our campuses and see the lost souls pinned-down, molested by the devil and on their way to eternal damnation.

In His great compassion, Jesus came to seek and save the lost. The word *save* in the Greek is *sozo*; it means "to heal, save, make well or whole."[7] The first and greatest miracle is always salvation. The greatest miracle happens when someone repents and commits their life to Christ. But to save (*sozo*) does not only mean to save the spirit; it also means to save the soul and body. Jesus' concern is to restore every part of a person's life. Our goal is not first to get to heaven but to bring heaven, which brings God's power to heal, down to earth.

Jesus healed the sick because His nature is compassion. And Jesus is the same, yesterday, today, and forever (see Heb. 13:8). Today He still desires to heal the sick. We follow Christ in doing greater works than Him (see John 14:12), such as healing, so that people will know the compassion of Jesus. Our nature must be like His. We must heal the sick because of love and for no other reason. We must be moved with compassion to operate in divine healing power to heal the sick and demonstrate the compassion of Jesus to this unbelieving generation. This is not a suggestion; it is a command of Jesus (see Matt. 10:1, 7-8; 28:20; Luke 9:1-2; 10:9).

Consider this: when Jesus was on earth, His purpose and work was to destroy the works of the devil (see 1 John 3:8). He did this by casting out demons, healing the sick, raising the dead, and preaching the Gospel of the kingdom. We must do the same. To preach the Gospel without casting out demons and healing the sick is not a full Gospel.

In Luke 10:9, Jesus commanded the seventy disciples to go into the towns and villages to heal the sick and pronounce that the kingdom of God has come. There is a significant link between divine healing and the kingdom of God. It is through divine healing that people recognize the authority of God's power and that the presence of His supernatural kingdom has come. If we want heaven on earth, we must expect signs and wonders to confirm the preaching of the Gospel. Miracles and divine healing are signs that the kingdom is near. We desperately need these signs in our evangelism on campuses today. However, it is up to us to release God's power for the lost to be saved. Jesus commanded:

> *Go into all the world and preach the gospel to every creature. He who believes and is baptized will be saved; but he who does not believe will be condemned. And these signs will follow those who believe: In My name they will cast out demons; they will speak with new tongues; they will take up serpents; and if they drink anything deadly, it will by no means hurt them;* **they will lay hands on the sick, and they will recover** *(Mark 16:15-18).*

The words of Jesus are clear: Those who preach the gospel, who believe and who are baptized, *will* cast out demons and heal the sick. This mandate is for all believers—for you and me. It isn't only for the apostle, the ordained minister, or the healing evangelist who will perform these signs, but for *everyone who believes* (see John 14:12). God has given us authority and power over sickness and disease. The Holy Spirit who was in the apostle Paul, who was in the apostle Peter, and who was in Smith Wigglesworth is the same Holy Spirit who is in us.

As you go out onto your campuses preaching the Gospel, look for the oppressed and look for sick people to heal. Hunt for the sick like a lion hunting for prey. The Word of God guarantees that He will show up: *"And they went out and preached everywhere, the Lord working with them and confirming the word through the accompanying signs"* (Mark 16:20). In our simple church network at UCLA we challenge our students to pray for one sick person each day on campus to be divinely healed. Almost every week we get email praise reports of divine encounters students have had when obeying the Holy Spirit to pray for the sick. Come on!

How to Pray for Divine Healing

There is much theology about divine healing, but I am not here to explain why God heals or doesn't heal today. I am here to say that I've seen it happen in my life, through my life, and to others time and time again for the sole purpose of glorifying Jesus.

It is clear that the Bible commands us to pray for the sick to be healed (see James 5:14-16). This is a grace available to every believer (see John 14:12; 1 Cor. 12:9). It is also clear that we are called to lay hands on the sick for their recovery (see Mark 16:18). Divine healing is a weapon in our arsenal to win the lost and bring revival. If we look throughout the Gospels and the book of Acts (see especially Acts 3:1-10, 5:12-16), divine healing was used by Jesus and the early disciples to gather large crowds, fill them with awe, and shake entire cities so that multitudes would be saved.

I asked a Baptist missionary friend of mine in China, "How is it that the Church in China is growing so fast?" He replied, "It is mainly through signs, wonders, miracles, and divine healing." God is releasing healing power in this hour and it's our responsibility to take it to our campuses. How do we use this spiritual weapon of divine healing power? My spiritual father, Pastor Ché Ahn, taught me how to pray for divine healing using the five steps below, that were originally developed by John Wimber and the Vineyard.[8]

As you go out onto campus each day, look for sick people to pray for. Whether it is a cold, a broken arm or leg, or a serious disease. Simply introduce yourself and ask them if you can pray for their divine healing, because you know that there is no prayer too big or too small that God can't answer. Then follow the below steps on how to pray for the sick...

Step 1: Investigate the Sickness

Find out what the sickness is by asking questions. Simply ask the sick person what is wrong with him or her. Where does it hurt? How did it happen? When did it happen? It is not our goal to know the details of the illness; we are not doctors. But we do want to investigate enough to know what we are praying for. Prayer must be specific. Peter and John told the lame man in Acts 3 to take up his mat and walk. They knew his sickness and, therefore, they were able to be specific in their prayer for his healing.

The sick person's response may be anything from, "I have a migraine" to "I just found out I have cancer." When I talked with the fraternity brother at UCLA, he told me exactly why he had crutches and a broken foot. By knowing what was wrong, I could pray for the divine healing with precision.

Step 2: Welcome the Holy Spirit

Once you know what the sickness is, invite the Holy Spirit into the situation before you engage in prayer: "Come Holy Spirit,[9] rest on this person and increase Your power on their body where they need healing." We can do nothing without the Holy Spirit and no healing can take place without the presence of the Holy Spirit to heal. For Jesus healed the paralytic man in the house in Capernaum, and the text of Luke 5:17 says, *"And the power of the Lord was present to heal them."*[10] As this verse suggests, the Holy Spirit must be manifestly present in order for the power of the Lord to be released for healing. It is Jesus that heals, not us. We simply partner with the Holy Spirit to bring about divine healing to others.

Step 3: Diagnostic Decision

Now find out the cause of the condition. What is causing this sickness? There are three main causes for sickness: 1) Physiological, 2) Demonic, and 3) Sin. Some people are sick because of natural circumstances. Maybe they caught a cold, got into an accident, or are not taking care of their health. Others may have a sickness where the root cause is demonic (see Matt. 12:22; Mark 9:17,25; Luke 11:14; 13:11).

There are also people who are sick because of hidden or harbored sin in their lives (see Luke 5:20,24-25). James 5:14-16 says:

Is anyone among you sick? Let him call for the elders of the church, and let them pray over him, anointing him with oil in the name of the Lord. And the prayer of faith will save the sick, and the Lord will raise him up. And if he has committed sins, he will be forgiven. Confess your trespasses to one another, and pray for one another, that you may be healed.

We are called to confess our sins to one another in order to be physically healed. Sin opens a door for sickness and the demonic to enter into our life (see Ps. 32:3-438:3,5; 1 Cor. 11:27-30; James 5:16).

There are five factors or types of sins that can cause sickness:

1. Sins of emotion and attitude, such as unbelief and pride.

2. Sins that we commit against others that cause bitterness and hatred in us, in the other person, or in both.

3. Sins that others commit against us, such as physical, verbal, or emotional abuse that may cause trauma and hurt and may open a door to satan.

4. Sins of our generational fathers: generational sins and curses. Exodus 20:5 says that the sins of the fathers are visited upon the children to the third and fourth generations. A child may be born with a disease, such as cancer, or may inherit a tendency such as a weakness toward alcoholism because their parent had the same condition or sinful tendency.

5. Sins that we commit against ourselves: self-hatred, self-rejection, inferiority complex, guilt, and condemnation.

A rule of thumb to follow when praying for divine healing: If the pain is recent due to an accident, it is most likely physiological; if the problem is chronic and the doctors have no answer for the cause, it could very well be demonic. If you ask Him, the Holy Spirit can give you discernment as to what the root cause of the problem is. Finally, if it is neither physiological nor demonic, sensitively ask the person you are praying for if they may have committed any sin to open the door for the sickness to occur. If there is sin committed, lead them in a prayer of repentance, then pray for healing.

Step 4: Select the Prayer Type

I generally use different kinds of prayer to apply to different causes of sickness. That day at UCLA, I used *command prayer* to command the student to rise up and walk. Jesus used command prayer most frequently in the Gospels.[11] Other times I will use rebuke prayer when I discern that the cause of sickness is demonic.[12] I'll pray, "In the name of Jesus I bind this spirit of infirmity and rebuke it out of this person's life now in Jesus name!" If the sickness is not healed immediately, I use intercessory prayer and simply pray, "Jesus I pray that You heal my friend of (name the sickness), in Jesus name. Amen."

Step 5: Pray

Once you have chosen a kind of prayer, invite the presence of the Holy Spirit and engage in prayer. I have learned to pray with my eyes open so I can discern what the Holy Spirit is doing. After praying, I will ask the person, "How do you feel?" Or I'll say, "Tell me what is going on now." Sometimes they are healed instantly; other times, nothing happens. If the healing does not immediately take place, I will ask the Holy Spirit how to continue in prayer, or whether there is a block to His anointing that I have not yet discovered. It is crucial that you follow the leading of the Holy Spirit throughout. Sometimes, I will continue with *intercessory prayer*, asking Jesus to heal and having the person soak in God's presence.

Once, during a healing meeting in LA, I heard the word "duck feet" and knew someone in the meeting had this problem. By faith, I gave the word of knowledge that there was someone in the room who needed to be healed of duck feet. In a room of about 200 students, suddenly one student walked up slowly to the platform. He had torsional deformities that caused his feet to point outward since birth. I prayed for him and nothing happened at first, but I prayed again and told him to soak in God's presence. Five minutes later he yelled out, "I'm healed." When we looked, his feet were completely straight, healed, and he began to walk normally all around the room praising God!

Step 6: Check the Healing and Give Post-Prayer Direction

It is important after praying for someone's healing to first have them check if they are healed. Ask them to try to do something they have not done before. Then give them post-prayer direction. You can tell the person to thank God for the healing. Even if they did not receive an instantaneous healing, encourage them to continually believe and thank God by faith for the healing (see Mark 11:22-24). Divine healing can be a process and may not always be immediate,[13] but as a general rule, it is the will of God to heal the sick. James 5:15 indicates that it is God's will to heal as a general rule: *"the prayer of faith **will heal the sick person"*** (the Greek future indicative *sosei* means "will heal" *not* "may heal" or "might heal if it's God's will").

The overall witness of the New Testament regarding God's attitude toward healing shows that God desires to heal. Any reader of the Gospels knows that God's Son, Jesus, healed the sick. Acts and the Epistles show that the apostles and Early Church also healed the sick. God gave the Church gifts of healing (see 1 Cor. 12:9), but He also commands the Church to pray for the sick in James 5:14-16. However, Scripture also makes it clear that in a minority of cases, for various reasons, the Early Church did not always see all the sick healed (see Gal. 4:13-14; Phil. 2:26-27; 1 Tim. 5:23; 2 Tim. 4:20).

So while Scripture makes it clear that it is generally God's will to heal, Scripture also shows us that we need to be ready for cases where for various reasons, people we pray for may not be healed over the short term or over the long term. And we need to keep in mind that there are many factors that can bring about or not bring about the healing. James 5:15 says that the *"prayer of faith will save the sick,"* indicating that the faith of those praying is the faith that is most important for healing to occur.

We need to encourage those who are not healed that it is not necessarily any lack of faith on their part that is preventing healing. Also, we need to encourage those we pray for to study and continually confess the promises concerning healing found in God's Word (see Isa. 53:5). Finally, if they receive a manifestation of healing, ask them to have it verified by a doctor. The student who walked off the crutches at Bruin Walk went to a doctor the next day to verify the healing, and the doctor was amazed at how quickly he recovered!

As we step out in faith to do what may seem ridiculous, God will do the miraculous. We do our part, which is to pray, and Jesus will do His part, which is to heal. It is not our job to heal; we only pray in the name of Jesus and expect God to show up. But, we must pray in faith believing for the sick to be healed, for whatever we ask for, if we believe we have received it, it will be ours (see Mark 11:24). In reality, we are called to "heal the sick" not just "pray for them" because it is an act of faith where Jesus heals through our obedience to His command (see Luke 10:9). I have prayed for many who were not healed instantly, but that has not deterred my passion to pray for the sick. We are to be a generation of faith, called to do "greater works" than even Jesus (see John 14:12). Step out in faith, go out two by two on your campus, look for the sick and pray for them by faith to be healed!

Holy Spirit, I pray that You will move this generation with deep compassion for the lost on our campuses and give us a burning passion to pray for the sick with divine healing power. In the name of Jesus.
Amen.

Endnotes

1. Chapter 11, *The Blueprint* by Jaeson Ma.

2. Smith Wigglesworth, *Greater Works: Experiencing God's Power* (New Kensington, PA: Whitaker House, 1999), n.p.

3. Roberts Liardon, ed., *Cry of the Spirit: Unpublished Sermons by Smith Wigglesworth* (Laguna Hills, CA: Embassy Publishing, 1991), 1, 10.

4. James Strong, *The New Strong's Exhaustive Concordance* (Nashville, TN: Thomas Nelson, 1984), Greek #4697.

5. Bauer et al., *A Greek-English Lexicon of the New Testament and Other Early Christian Literature*, 762.

6. See the original meaning of the Greek word *skullo*, "to flay, to skin," in Ibid., p. 758; see the meanings of the Greek word *ripto* in Ibid., 736.

7. Ibid., p. 798; James Strong, *The New Strong's Exhaustive Concordance* (Nashville, TN: Thomas Nelson, 1984) Greek #4982.

8. Ché Ahn, *How to Pray for Divine Healing* (Ventura: Regal Books, 2004), p. 129; John Wimber and Kevin Springer, *Power Healing*. San Francisco: Harper and Row, 1987.

9. In Hebrew, the phrase for "Come Holy Spirit" is *bo'i haruakh*; see Ezekiel 37:9; Psalm 141:1, "O Lord, I call to you; come quickly to me" (NIV); 2 Corinthians 3:17, "Now the Lord *is the Spirit*" (emphasis added).

10. The Holy Spirit is always with us (see Ps. 139:7-10; John 14:16-19). But He comes specially and manifests distinctive anointing for particular purposes according to the following passages: Luke 5:17, "the power of the Lord *was present* to heal," implying that there were times when the power of the Lord *was not present*; 1 Corinthians 5:4, "When...the power of the Lord Jesus"; Isaiah 55:6, "Seek the Lord *while He may be found*; call upon Him *while He is near*."

11. Examples of command prayer:

"Be clean!" (to a leper), Mark. 1:41, NIV.

"Get up!" (to a lame man), Mark 2:11, NIV; John 5:8, NIV; Acts 9:34, NIV.

"Stretch out your hand," Mark 3:5.

"Get up" (to a dead person), Mark 5:41, NIV; Luke 7:14, NIV; Acts 9:40, NIV.

"Be opened!" (to a deaf man's ears), Mark 7:34.

Jesus "rebuked the fever, and it left her," Luke 4:39.

"See again! [Greek *Anablepson*]" (to a blind man), Luke 18:42.

"Lazarus, come forth!" John 11:43.

"Walk!" (to a lame man), Acts 3:6.

"Stand up!" (to a lame man), Acts 14:10.

12. An example of rebuke prayer: "Be quiet!...Come out of him!" (Mark 1:25).

13. See Mark 8:22-25, where Jesus had to lay hands more than once on the blind man before he was completely healed.

NOTES AND APPLICATIONS

Chapter 5

WHY GOD HEALS TODAY!

Marc A. Dupont

OF ALL THE ASPECTS AND FACETS of the ministry of Jesus Christ, none is more spectacular, and few are as controversial, as the healings and miracles that He performed and is still performing today. No small amount of controversy surrounded His supernatural acts while He walked the face of the earth in bodily form. If anything, probably more controversy surrounds the supernatural acts that He is doing today through His contemporary disciples by the power and leading of the Holy Spirit.

The modern day controversy exists for two essential reasons. First, it is rooted in the age-old disbelief in God and in Christ Jesus, His only begotten Son who came to earth to make known the Father and to make payment (atonement) for the sins of all who would choose to follow Him. Second, and probably more powerful, is the pharisaical unbelief from many of the *people of God*—those you would expect to have the most faith and excitement toward the supernatural demonstration of God's power and compassion.

The Power of Unbelief

Before we delve into why God is still, today, in the healing business, I would like to briefly discuss the power of unbelief that exists among many in the Church. I believe it needs to be understood because, just as unbelief sometimes proved to be a very real barrier between needy people and the release of healing in Jesus' day (see Matt. 13:58), so it can be today!

Since the beginning of humanity, the huge temptation has been to limit our understandings, perspectives, and faith levels to what we can humanly perceive as rational. This temptation first manifested when the serpent persuaded Eve to eat of the tree of knowledge of good and evil with the lie that, if she partook of it, she could be "as God" (see Gen. 3:4-5). The lie was that they, Adam and Eve, could be in control of life and destiny without needing a dependence on and an overriding trust in the person of God.

When Eve, and subsequently Adam, ate of the tree of knowledge of good and evil, knowledge was gained, but the cost was horrific. Humanity lost the place and possibility of intimacy with God until thousands of years later when Christ came and gave His life on the cross. Adam and Eve, as representatives of humanity, were subsequently cast out of the Garden—a place of intimacy with God and a place of great beauty and nurturing where all of their needs were met.

After The Fall, they landed in the world where they lacked intimacy with God, survived life by the *"sweat of their brow"* (Gen. 3:19), lacked eternal life and health, and experienced perpetual conflict with everything else, including fellow humans. The prize that they gained—a greater intellectual knowing—turned out to be a poor swap for God's immediate presence, provision, and protection.

This demonically-inspired transaction, unfortunately, set the stage for the greatest battle of history, one that humanity still continually faces. It is the battle between a simple trust in the person of God and His goodness and a dependence on our own understanding as we strive to be in control and to be responsible for ourselves and our destinies.

Two Lies

In a word, pride, especially, the pride of life, became one of the two greatest demonic strongholds over humanity. The pride of life is when we glory in what we have accomplished and fail to give God thanks and praise for creating, gifting, and enabling us. One of the greatest strongholds of pride is intellectualism devoid of a proper regard for God. The apostle Paul warned that knowledge apart from living for Christ brings about arrogance (see 1 Cor. 8:1b), which is an affront to God. God, the greatest intellectual of all, created us to be intellectuals. After all, we are created in His image. The question, however, is whether that intellect flows out of a childlike relationship with God or out of an aloofness from God.

The other stronghold, which goes hand-in-hand with the pride of life, is a disbelief that God wants to be personally and directly involved with human beings. This came about as Adam and Eve bought into the insinuating lie that satan posed as a question when he said, *"Did God really say...."* (Gen. 3:1). It should be noted that, with both of these great lies, the devil came as a serpent. A snake does not rush on its victims with great noise or fanfare. Rather, he comes in with both subtleness and an almost seductive beauty. The chief lies gripping humanity today, which war against a living relationship with God are both subtle and seductive in regard to our intellect and pride.

Enter, Jesus

In contrast to the almost all-encompassing pride of life and disbelief in God's goodness, along came Jesus of Nazareth. He spoke, healed, loved, lived, and ate with a simplicity and goodness that confounded the religious leaders of His day. The simplicity of His wisdom and ways confronted the pride and religious posturing that surrounded the priests and political leaders.

When Jesus performed the great miracles, He demonstrated almost a complete lack of sophistication in how He prayed. Those leaders were offended that He did these outrageous acts of compassion without even jumping through the hoops of protocol and tradition that they so highly valued. Further, He often completely ignored their valued head knowledge about things they considered highly important. In contrast to their teaching, He sometimes ate without washing the hands, He healed people on the Sabbath day, and He allowed women—including women of questionable reputation—to be in His presence (see Matt. 15:1-20; 12:9-14; Luke 7:37-39).

Their problem was (and it is our problem too) that, because they had lost a simple trust in the person and presence of God, they placed a great emphasis on their knowledge of right and wrong and on their traditions of religion. In contrast to Jesus, and even in contrast to the Scriptures that they were so apt to quote, they leaned to their own understanding (see Prov. 3:5).

In a simple, yet powerful statement (which offends our reliance on sophistication, man-made traditions, and our limited understanding), Jesus stated that one must be both converted and become like a child in order to experience the Kingdom of God (see Mark 10:15; Luke 18:17). Of course, He did not say become *childish*, but rather to be *childlike,* to return to childlike trust and dependence on the person of God.

He also openly challenged the prideful belief that somehow we can earn or achieve the blessings of God. When asked, *"What shall we do, that we may work the works of God?" Jesus answered and said to them, "This is the work of God, that you believe in Him whom He sent"* (John 6:28-29). His answer offends the pride of man. Surely the blessings of God are something we can earn or achieve, aren't they? It took a prophet, speaking by the Spirit of God, to proclaim and realize that the best righteousness that we can truly achieve by our own ability is as a filthy rag compared to God's goodness (see Isa. 64:6).

These two lies, which have become entrenched in the soul of humanity—trust in our own understanding (abilities) and disbelief in God's desire to truly have personal relationship with us—stood as an almost insurmountable wall against responding positively to the in-your-face goodness of Jesus. Unfortunately, those same two strongholds still hold sway over much of the Church in the western world today.

The Lies Today

No one comes to Christ without an authentic heart revelation of the reality that Jesus is the Christ. However, a large portion of the contemporary Body of Christ accepts that miracle of God's love, including the resurrection from the dead, but allows the same old lies to govern their beliefs about what God wants to do today. I believe this is because it is easier to accept healings, miracles, signs, and wonders that happened long ago and that historians and eye-witnesses testify about. If we believe that God is doing the same sort of miracles and healings today, then we must deal with our mindsets and change our paradigms in order to facilitate the near-ness and radical goodness of God. It is one thing to say, "Jesus healed the blind two thousand years ago." It is almost another thing entirely to say, "Not only did Jesus heal the blind two thousand years ago, but because He is the same yesterday, today, and forever (see Heb. 13:8), He wants to do the same right now."

Jesus also dealt with this sort of juxtapositioning of eternal and spiritual authority against authority in contemporary life. In Mark 2, we read that four friends carried a fifth friend, who was paralyzed, to Jesus. While it is clear from the Gospel accounts that not all sick-ness and disease is due to personal or generational sin (see John 9:2-3), there is evidence that it occasionally is (see John 5:14). In the case of this paralyzed man, we don't know for sure what the cause of His lameness was, but Jesus, seeing the faith of his friends (faith is always a necessity for accessing God's goodness), proclaimed, *"Son, your sins are forgiven you"* (Mark 2:5).

Immediately Jesus became aware that the scribes present were grumbling in their hearts. He responded to them, *"But that you may know that the Son of Man has power on earth to forgive sins"—He said to the paralytic, "I say to you, arise, take up your bed, and go to your house"* (Mark 2:10-11). The man was immediately healed. Jesus graphically and unambiguously shut down all immediate argument concerning whether or not He truly walked in God's authority. Healings and miracles today, just as in the time of Jesus, are quite powerful in demonstrating and proving the present real-ity of God's Kingdom. Someone with a true Holy Spirit experience is no longer at the mercy of someone with a pharisaical argument. As the blind man healed by Jesus in John 9 said, when questioned by the Pharisees, *"...One thing I know: that though I was blind, now I see"* (John 9:25).

The Church today would do well to realize that, if we claim spiritual authority in representing Christ, we should demonstrate that authority in the natural realm, just as Jesus did.

Two Essential Reasons

In this section, I will address the two greatest reasons, according to the Bible, why God still performs healings and miracles today. Both reasons are the complete antithesis of the lies that humanity embraced in the Garden of Eden.

One: God's Goodness

In complete contrast to the normal condition of humanity, God is good. In fact, His goodness is beyond our understanding. His very essence is a heart of compassion that is full of grace, slow to become angry, and rich in loving-kindness and truth (see Exod. 34:6). When a man addressed Jesus as a "good teacher," Jesus responded, "*Why do you call Me good? No one is good except God alone*" (Luke 18:19 NASB). In other words, Jesus was saying that the goodness that He demonstrated was only possible if He was truly God and not just a man trying to do good works. Any human involved in charitable, kind, and encouraging works is a reflection of the nature of God. But even at our best, we fail to *truly* represent the awesomeness of God's goodness.

I remember one particular miracle I saw the Lord perform while I was ministering in the African bush. While I was preaching about Jesus from a small wooden platform with a portable sound system and generator, a small group of drunken men off to the side of the crowd began mocking me, my preaching, and the message of the Gospel.

After I finished preaching, we entered a ministry time, and I had an impression from the Holy Spirit to call up people for healing who had bad legs. One of the drunken men immediately had his friends help him up, and he hobbled over to the platform on crutches made out of tree limbs.

After a few moments of prayer, the man was completely healed of over 10 years of lameness. They brought him up to the platform, and even while drunk, he and others testified to the complete healing. While in the army, fighting the communist regime years earlier, a soldier in front of him had stepped on a land mine. That soldier died instantly, and this man's leg was filled with shrapnel. He had been lame ever since. After testifying about the healing, he decided to give his life to Christ Jesus.

Late that night, before going to bed, I prayed. While I was excited about that healing and the others that had happened, I was a bit surprised that the Lord had healed this man while he was mocking the Gospel message and even mocking Jesus. While praying, my heart was drawn to this passage:

"For My thoughts are not your thoughts, nor are your ways My ways," declares the Lord. For as the heavens are higher than the earth, so are My ways higher than your ways and My thoughts than your thoughts (Isaiah 55:8-9 NASB).

When God told Moses that He is a God of compassion and grace (see Exod. 34:6), He did not mean goodness according to human standards. Rather, He spoke of a degree of compassion, goodness, grace, and mercy that is alien to unredeemed humanity.

But Jesus demonstrated for us God's compassion and goodness while on earth. In the accounts of His miracles, both physical healings and multiplication of food, many times it indicates that Jesus was motivated by *compassion* (see Mark 1:41; Matt. 15:32-39; 20:30-34; Luke 7:12-15).

Of all of the parables that Jesus told, the story of the prodigal son most poignantly illustrates the heart of God (see Luke 15:11-32). The good father sees his wayward son walking toward him *"when he was still a great way off"* (Luke 15:20). The son epitomizes shame, guilt, poverty, and brokenness. But the father, with no regard for the shame that the son had brought to him, *"had compassion, and ran and fell on his neck and kissed him"* (Luke 15:20).

A grown man in that culture, unless in battle, would never run publicly due to the embarrassment of having to pull up his robe, thus revealing his undergarments.[1] The father of the prodigal son, however, was prodigal in his love for his son. The word *prodigal,* which isn't part of the manuscripts of the Gospel, is a Latin word that essentially means "wastefully extravagant." Likewise, God the Father extravagantly gave Jesus as a sacrifice in order to redeem and restore us.

God's nature never changes; He still heals today. And He has instructed us to *"preach, saying, 'The kingdom of heaven is at hand.' Heal the sick, cleanse the lepers, raise the dead, cast out demons..."* (Matt. 10:7-8).

Two: Evangelism

The contemporary western Church's primary evangelistic tools have been preaching and teaching. This starkly contrasts the early Church and the Church today in Africa, South America, and much of Asia. These groups utilized both the word (preaching) and the *works of power* by the Holy Spirit.

According to the apostle Paul, who moved prolifically in signs, wonders, and the miraculous, the Kingdom of God does not consist merely of words, but of power (see 1 Cor. 4:20). Specifically, Paul wrote of *dunamis* ("dynamite") power. This dynamite power is the same sort of power that Jesus promised to the disciples (see Acts 1:8).

Jesus' Power Ministry

Jesus also emphasized miraculous works. In fact, in John 10, Jesus defended Himself by saying:

> *If I do not do the works of My Father, do not believe Me; but if I do, though you do not believe Me, believe the works, that you may know and believe that the Father is in Me, and I in Him* (John 10:37-38).

In other words, Jesus told the people that the miracles, healings, signs, and wonders that He performed spoke for themselves, identifying Him as the Son of God.

Jesus expected the Jews to understand the connection between His identity and His demonstration of the Kingdom of God. If He was healing blindness, deafness, lameness, and leprosy, then Heaven was truly invading earth and He must be the Messiah.

When John the Baptist was imprisoned and soon to be martyred, He sent his disciples to Jesus for assurance. They said to Jesus:

> *"Are You the Expected One, or shall we look for someone else?" Jesus answered and said to them, "Go and report to John what you hear and see: the blind receive sight and the lame walk, the lepers are cleansed and the deaf hear, the dead are raised up, and the poor have the gospel preached to them* (Matthew 11:2-5 NASB).

Notice what Jesus *did not say*. He did not say "Yes, I am the Messiah," or "Take John my 18-point doctoral thesis." He simply told them to relate the Kingdom works of power that were taking place.

Paul's Power Ministry

The apostle Paul's ministry was foremost in releasing revival in the known world of his day. He also wrote (under the inspiration of the Holy Spirit) some of the most important theological writings of the New Testament, including the book of Romans.

But Paul, the outstanding apostle, theologian, evangelist, and worker-of-miracles, placed no weight on his own speaking or oratory abilities. (This contrasts the emphasis placed on the verbal presentation of the preacher, speaker, or teacher in the contemporary Church.)

If Paul, one of the most powerful and effective apostles, placed little importance on his speaking abilities and personal presentation, what did he attribute his effectiveness to? He wrote to the church of Corinth:

*My message and my preaching were not in persuasive words of wisdom, but in demonstration of the Spirit and of **power**, so that your faith would not rest on the wisdom of men, but on the **power** of God (1 Corinthians 2:4-5 NASB).*

To Paul, the sign of an authentic apostolic ministry was not clever, persuasive sermons but the demonstration of healings, miracles, signs, and wonders.

Clearly, Jesus and the early apostles demonstrated the Kingdom with power—and that power was the key to spreading the Gospel.

Modern Power Ministry

As I have been saying all along, God is still using power ministry today. On many occasions, I have had the privilege of seeing people come to Christ after experiencing a touch of God's supernatural power. In fact, I have even occasionally seen a majority of the population of small African bush villages come to Christ when a villager was miraculously healed.

Several years ago, before I started a series of meetings in Malmoe, Sweden, I was taken to the house of a lady belonging to the church. Her husband, who at that time had no relationship with Christ, was dying from cancer of the stomach. I joined with their grown children and a few of their friends in a time of prayer for his healing. While not much seemed to happen at that time, I found out over a year later that, within a few weeks, he had a complete, miraculous recovery from the cancer. As a result, he, as well as his grown children, began attending church and growing closer to God.

Recently, while I was ministering in a church in northern England, I had the opportunity to pray for a teenage girl who had been living out in the streets. Among other problems, she suffered from Hepatitis C. One of the pastors, who had been reaching out to young girls on the street, brought her up for prayer when I gave a word of knowledge about blood disorders. As I began to pray for her, not only did I sense God's healing power come on her, but I also sensed the Lord directing me to tell her that God had incredible plans for her life.

A few weeks after returning home, I received an email from that pastor, telling me the good news. The medical report had come back with amazing results. She no longer had Hepatitis C! The pastor now had an open door to begin counseling and praying with her to come to Christ and to enter into her destiny in God. What that girl needed was not just words of life, but the life-changing power of God's compassion, as well.

Such power ministry is often much more common in the non-western Church. But many in ministry today, including me, long to see God's power moving in western nations as it does in parts of Africa and Asia. The good news is that miraculous healings, signs, and wonders are on the increase today in places such as North America, the UK, and Europe.

So why has the western Church fallen behind in demonstrations of the Kingdom in power? Unfortunately, much of the contemporary Church in the West has limited herself to words alone. We have adopted a sub-representation of the compassion and authority of God. We need to return to a reliance on the person and power of the Holy Spirit.

Some may argue that what worked in the ancient cultures or what works today in some third world cultures will not work in our western world. To a degree, that may be true—there is far more faith in many of the cultures of Africa, Asia, and South America. I have seen over 60 percent of a bush village in Africa come to Christ because of a few miracles.

Certainly we are not yet experiencing that sort of fruit from the demonstration of God's Kingdom in North America or Europe. But I have seen entire families, including extended family members, come to Christ through one family member being healed of cancer or other serious illnesses in both Europe and North America.

Regardless of our cultural differences, healings and miracles are one of God's ways of demonstrating and releasing His compassion and Kingdom. If we want to see biblical results from biblical actions (preaching the Gospel), we need to do things God's way.

According to H.B. London, of Focus on the Family, over the last 20 years, 500 billion dollars has been spent on ministry in the United States with no real noticeable effect on the nation.[2] Mere words and programs, as important as they are, simply are not enough.

Jesus promised:

*Truly, truly, I say to you, he who believes in Me, the works that I do, he will do also; and **greater works** than these he will do; because I go to the Father* (John 14:12 NASB).

People desperately need God's healing compassion and power. And the same King who looked on the multitudes and healed them because He felt compassion on them 2000 years ago cares deeply for the multitudes today.

Let me share one final example of God's power serving to open someone up to the reality of the Gospel; it took place in Scotland several years ago. A woman in the church had been led by God to reach out to young girls on the street. She brought three street girls along to one of the meetings that I was doing. Church, Christianity, and God, Himself, were completely outside of their experience. At the end of the meeting, I called up people with learning disabilities for prayer. The lady from the church brought up one of the street girls who suffered from severe dyslexia. After a few moments of prayer, I opened my Bible up to Leviticus, which can be difficult to read out loud, even for someone without dyslexia. She was able to read perfectly! She was in tears as she related that normally she could hardly read three words in a row without stumbling. She, too, came to Christ due to experiencing the kindness of God which leads people to repentance (see Rom. 2:4).

In conclusion, I'm reminded of what the writer of the Book of Hebrews wrote, under the inspiration of the Holy Spirit: *"Jesus*

Christ is the same yesterday, today, and forever" (see Heb. 13:8). Because of who He is, He desires to do the same things today as He did over two thousand years ago.

Endnotes

1. Matthew Poole, *Matthew Poole's Commentary* vol. 1 (Peabody, MA: Hendrickson Publishers, 1982), on Job 38:3 and Exodus 28:42-43.

2. *Pastor's Briefing*, February 22, 1999.

NOTES AND APPLICATIONS

Chapter 6

POWER EVANGELISM
AND GOD'S NATURE

Graham Cooke

WHAT WE THINK ABOUT GOD is the most important issue in the world. Perception is everything. When Jesus asked the question *"Who do men say that I, the Son of Man, am?"* (Matt. 16:13), He was not fishing for a compliment. He was asking a vital question concerning identity. The answer He received showed that He was not perceived properly and, therefore, could not be received effectively.

There were four distorted images in the perceptions of people concerning Jesus. To some, He was John the Baptist, a reincarnation obviously, since John had been murdered by Herod. Others were of the opinion that He was Elijah or Jeremiah reborn. Less specifically, some people saw Him as "one of the prophets."

When He made the same question personal to His disciples, He was checking out their testimony. *"Who do you say that I am"* (Matt. 16:15). Our testimony is not about what we were like before we met Jesus. That is our history. Our testimony is: "This is who Jesus is to me; this is how He relates to me; this is what He is like to me…all the time." Testimony is about the consistency of truth in our experience. This is what Jesus is like. This is how He shows up in my life. We are witnesses to His nature first, then to His redemptive power.

There are many distorted images about God in the Church, so it is hardly surprising that the world has a negative understanding of the nature of God. If we are to become wonderful ambassadors of reconciliation, then we need to understand the nature of harmony. To reconcile means to restore the harmony between two people in conflict.

Reconciliation cannot occur until someone is willing to trust. The nature of evangelism, therefore, is to establish a place in the hearts of people where trust can take place. People require some evidence of the others' intention. All relationships of worth and value are built upon the nature and character of the people involved. Where there is conflicting evidence of character and intentionality, trust is not possible.

The nature of God is a bigger issue than the power of God. In desperate circumstances, people will avail themselves of any power, regardless of source, if it will alleviate their condition or the suffering of a loved one. However, we do not build relationships with a power source. Therefore, the question "what is God really, really like?" is most vital. Witnessing is not an event; it is a lifestyle. We wear our relationship with God for all to see.

We are learning how to live like the Father, perceive as He does, act in line with His goodness, speak from His heart, and think in alignment with His kindness. How we perceive God is how we will live and act toward others.

Authentic Intimacy

This is the Christ that I have personally encountered on my journey of life. He has an immense, immeasurable, and eternal compassion. His compassion is always greater than our sin. He is scandalously forgiving. His mercy burns as it destroys shame. He has unbounded patience, unending goodness.

His love is so compelling that it heals us. It strips away all of our pretense and restores us to happiness. His grace is so incredible that we are empowered to feel good about ourselves while we are in the process of becoming more Christlike. His mercy is His total favor, given gladly to the undeserving heart.

He is the kindest person I have ever known. His goodness is so outrageous and shocking; it is actually disreputable to the religious-minded. He is the happiest person I know. He has the sunniest disposition imaginable! He is enthusiastically fervent in His pursuit of us. He is amazingly humble and gentle, but He is also a powerful warrior king who loves to fight and laughs at His enemies.

He has a fabulous servant spirit, needing no title, status, or position as a man; He joyfully sets an example of simple, heart-warming servanthood. His love is enthralling. It captivates us and commands us to be full of loving kindness. His love is designed to overwhelm all things, especially fear, shame, and low self-esteem. He loves being trusted. He is delightful and astonished when we use our faith.

He will never keep a record of our sins or failings. He has mercy that can never be properly understood or articulated, just experienced! The only way that we can explain mercy is by being merciful ourselves. Jesus the Redeemer gives us value in the eyes of the Father. He sees and speaks to our potential. He both protects us and releases us to fulfill all that He wants us to see and know about ourselves.

Obviously, that is but a fraction of what I have seen, heard, and known by experience. Our lives are profoundly shaped by our experience of Jesus. Our conversations about God reflect our experiences of Him. We are first-hand witnesses regarding how God moves in our lives and who He is for us in any given circumstance.

We are designed and created to reflect God's beauty. To that end, He desires that we live in His presence and know Him powerfully by experience. The authenticity of our intimacy provokes people to see who God is in reality. Our enjoyment of God is our best source of inspirational witness.

One thing I have desired of the Lord, that will I seek: that I may dwell in the house of the Lord all the days of my life, to behold the beauty of the Lord, and to inquire in His temple" (Psalm 27:4).

The love of God surely is the gift of Himself. All other gifts pale in comparison to the glory of Who He is, alive in His people. We get to enjoy our Creator. We actually gain Christ! We are at our absolute best when we are witnesses to His glorious nature. Giving the world a radiant idea of God actually elevates our identity in Christ.

We live a life of celebration. The Gospel of salvation in Christ is the foundation of our inner happiness. We live in the splendor of God's goodness. We are embraced by glory. His presence is so wonderful: *"...we rather to be absent from the body and to be present with the Lord"* (2 Cor. 5:8). Paul's desire was to depart and be with Christ, for that is far better (see Phil. 1:23).

Joyful Proclamation

The Gospel can only be proclaimed in fullness. Good news of great joy is that we can be saved to the uttermost—not just our souls, but our bodies, minds, emotions, and households. The very substance of our lives comes under this so great salvation. Every single aspect of life is redeemable. Christ the redeemer overwhelms all that is against us in life. *"...On earth as it is in Heaven"* was the way He came praying (Matt. 6:10). And *"...as He is, so are we in this world"* (1 John 4:17).

The angel of the Lord announced good news of an incredible joy (see Luke 2:10-11). Literally, it was a message regarding an astonishing victory. Heaven came down to celebrate the glorious outcome concerning the defeat of sin and all its consequences. Health and wholeness were being restored at all levels to mankind through Emmanuel. Fallen man could now become risen and ascended in Christ. Heaven had entered earth's atmosphere. The prince of the power of the air was to be thrown down, and God's people were given authority over all things through the Christ.

There can be no explanation of truth without first a proper proclamation of the Christ. Life in Jesus is a continuous act of celebration. We are restored to joy through salvation—the sheer pleasure in being saved and belonging to the Lord. Explanation is the unpacking of truth about the radiant nature of life in Christ. Proclamation makes us astonished at the goodness of God. We marvel in Him. By contrast, doctrine (explanation of truth) without proclamation is dull.

Doctrine should be rooted in awe and a sense of wonder. It should release worship, praise, rejoicing, and thanksgiving. Proclamation must have a prime place in a celebratory lifestyle. The goal of the Holy Spirit is the supreme exaltation of Jesus Christ. It is the revelation of the glory of Christ in the face of God. We are transformed by glory (see 2 Cor. 3:18). When we have a radiant idea of God, the glory of that revelation must lead us into an experience of the Lord so profound that the very substance of our life is altered.

A Radiant Idea of God

Beholding the glory of the Lord is a vital part of our life and witness. We are stunned by the radiant nature of God's personality. We are overcome, undone, and astonished to have a life in Christ. That radiant light changes our very personality (see 2 Cor. 4:6). As we look at Jesus, we are changed into His image. The Holy Spirit will always glorify Jesus (see John 16:14). He magnifies Christ in such a way as to cause amazement in our hearts. We laugh; we cry tears of joy; we are speechless in awe; we shout aloud at His majesty. Glory compels us to be extreme, to go beyond our innate personality in pursuing a suitable expression of worship.

It is the same when we preach, witness, and talk about Jesus. Our language is never general. It is always specific to our story, our testimony with a smile. The nature of God is always glorious. We change into what we most adore about God. Worship is vital to transformation. God seeks worshipers because intimate love, affection, and adoration are the best seed-bed for personal transformation. Rejoicing provokes renewal.

In Christ we get a perspective on life, events, and the world that is rooted in Heaven. The most earthly good is established by the most heavenly-minded people. Degrees of glory should be a commonplace experience for every child of God. Transformation is incremental. We get to taste the goodness of God on an ongoing basis. His Name is wonderful because it best describes the life that we have in Him. What would it be like to become conformed to glory?

It means that we see everything through the eyes of Jesus. His beauty affects us in every way. We live with such confident expectation of the Kingdom coming to earth in our hearts, our homes, our communities. We do what Jesus does because we are captured by His heart for us. The Holy Spirit trains us in glory. We look to Him and our faces are radiant (see Ps. 34:5). We sparkle with joy. We learn to be cheerful and develop the courage that arises out of a cheerful disposition. God is in control in Christ. He has overcome, and joyful courage is a very real possibility as a lifestyle (see John 16:33). It becomes our testimony and our witness. "This is what Jesus is like to me all the time." We are loved exactly as Jesus is loved by the Father (see John 17:23).

We are renewed daily in our inner person, even though age is catching up with us (see 2 Cor. 4:16-18). The Gospel must relate to glory, or it becomes just ordinary. Our experience must relate to glory, for we are the evidence of a radiant life. We are a demonstration, a visual aid to the earth, of the richness and beauty of God in Christ.

Authentic story creates confidence. It grabs the attention of people and influences their minds and hearts. Interest turns to desire and pursuit. Seeking takes place, and discovery is the result. The Father loves discovery. In His heart, seeking always carries a guarantee (see Luke 11:9). That alone should make us cheerful! Our testimony releases the power of experience to another.

This is true regardless of whether our testimony of God is positive or negative. Millions of people have accepted Christ as their personal savior because of the power of testimony leading them to desire a similar experience. Just as many people have rejected

Christ because they have been presented with a negative view of the nature of God.

Mercy Triumphs Over Judgment

It is difficult for the modern Church to rise up when we have made God in our own image. He has been invested with human attributes, and we are unable to experience His divine presence as a result. When the Father is portrayed as angry, judgmental, and capricious, then humanity has nothing to look up to and sin increases.

What we think about God determines our closeness to Him. The lack of real worship across the whole Church is devastatingly obvious. We have left our first love (see Rev. 2:4). Perhaps the sin of evangelicalism is that we have put the Great Commission ahead of the First Commandment. Across the spiritual community, as a whole, we have placed more value on service to, rather than intimacy with, the Father. Another thing to recover is our understanding of, experience of, and allegiance to the Kingdom of God first, rather than to our particular tribal designation.

If we perceive God as hard to know, difficult to relate to, and impossible to hear, then we will have relational problems. If we cannot hear someone's voice, then we must use sign language. But we are a community always looking for signs and ever failing to interpret them correctly.

The world has a picture of God supplied by the Church. If we are to experience a reformation, that image needs to be upgraded. God is not judging the world. He sent Jesus to save it.

For God did not send the Son into the world to judge the world, but that the world might be saved through Him (John 3:17 NASB).

You judge according to the flesh; I am not judging anyone (John 8:15 NASB).

I can do nothing on My own initiative. As I hear, I judge; and My judgment is just because I do not seek My own will, but the will of Him who sent me (John 5:30 NASB).

The questions we must ask ourselves about Jesus are these:

- Was Jesus judged enough? Clearly, if judgment is a part of the Church's ministry to the world, then Jesus died in vain. He was merely judged partially, and our salvation has no value.

- Was Jesus punished enough for sin? If the answer is affirmative, then grace can abound to all mankind, regardless of iniquity.

- Did the Father pour out every last ounce of anger and wrath upon Jesus? If so, then He has none left surely.

The reality is that God was in Christ reconciling the world to Himself, not counting their trespasses against them. And He has committed to us the word of reconciliation. Therefore, we are ambassadors for Christ. As a reconciled people, we enjoy all of the blessing and favor of being in the Kingdom, and we have been given the ministry of reconciliation to the world (see 2 Cor. 5:14-21).

Blessed are those whose lawless deeds have been forgiven, and whose sin has been covered. Blessed is the man to whom the Lord shall not impute sin (Romans 4:7-8).

The Father is not obsessed with sin; He dealt with it, once and for all, in Christ (see Rom. 6:10). Between Calvary—which was judgment on Christ for our sin—and the Day of Judgment—when the books will be opened—there is no place for judgment in this life.

*If anyone hears My sayings and does not keep them, I do not judge him; for I did not come to judge the world, but to save the world. He who rejects Me and does not receive My sayings has one who judges him; the word I spoke is what will judge him **at the last day*** (John 12:47-48 NASB).

Between Calvary and the Day of Judgment, we are living in a prophetic season of grace. As ambassadors of reconciliation, we judge the world by bringing the grace, mercy, and goodness of God into all of our relationships and communities.

It is the goodness and kindness of God that leads people to repentance (see Rom. 2:4). To be sure, a warning about the effects and consequences of sin upon our current lives is sound advice. A word pronouncing judgment is a condemnation of the Cross and its power to save in this present life. It is an abuse of authority, outside of the character of Christ and misaligned with our ambassadorial role of reconciliation.

Like Jesus, we must judge in a way that pleases the Father (see John 5:30). When we see someone steeped in sin, we are judging how much grace, mercy, and goodness it will take in order for them to see God as He really is and to respond to Him personally. We must operate in the world just as we are required to in the Church:

Brethren, even if anyone is caught in any trespass, you who are spiritual, restore such a one in a spirit of gentleness; each one looking to yourself, so that you too will not be tempted. Bear one another's burdens, and thereby fulfill the law of Christ (Galatians 6:1-2 NASB).

The Good News is that the world has been reconciled to God through Christ. The way is open for them to receive forgiveness, blessing, and favor. They are reconciled to God; His heart is open to receive them. In their fallen state, they can be given a divine standing in Christ.

It's like receiving a credit card in the mail. All the benefits and advantages are present, but they cannot be activated until we get in touch with the principle. As ambassadors, our role is to give people a taste and a look at the power of the Kingdom. We introduce them to the nature of God.

Radically and Wonderfully Loved

Our relationships are formed out of perceptions—not just what we think about the other person but also how we perceive they think about us. How we see God and how He sees us are key factors in our communication of the Gospel.

I love God with all my heart. I love the fact that He is love. His love never fails. It is not based on my performance as a Christian. There is nothing I can do that would make the Father love me more, and there is nothing I can do that would make Him love me less. Love is how He shows up in everything. He loves me in exactly the same way He loves Jesus (see John 17:23-26), and Jesus loves me in the same way that He is loved by the Father (see John 15:9).

I love God because He is faithful and unchanging. That makes Him a totally dependable life source. I always know where I am in His great heart because He never changes. I love His goodness, grace, and mercy. I adore His loving kindness and generosity. I appreciate enormously His gentle patience. I am overwhelmed by His joy and cheerfulness, and His peace and rest thrill me each day. I love His calm wisdom and His wild enthusiasm for me. I am humbled by His devotion as a Father and by the sheer size of His commitment to me in Christ. I love His acceptance of me in my struggle to be a better man. I love His favor and blessing as I process my journey with Him.

I love the fact that He is present future with me and not present past. He has dealt with my past, and my relationship with Him is about me discovering the plans that He has to give me a future and a hope (see Jer. 29:11). I love being encouraged by Him to forget what lies behind, to reach out for what lies ahead, and to press on toward the goal for the prize of the upward call of God in Christ Jesus (see Phil. 3:13-14).

I love the fact that, on my journey with Him, when He touches a part of my life that is not working properly, He is actually pointing out the site of my next miracle. I hear His voice, sometimes gentle, at other times cheerful, "Let's work on this together." I am a house being lovingly restored by a wise master builder. He understands me, sees me, and gets who I am. I feel loved in every part of my life. This is my witness. I am radically and wonderfully loved.

When I express the nature of my relationship with God to people who do not know Him, the radiance of my testimony reveals to them their own spiritual and human condition. We convict the world by the presence of God in us. We are sent out from the throne of grace. The best judgment is in self-awareness. *"...I am a man of unclean lips..."* (Isa. 6:5). *"...My sin is always before me"* (Ps. 51:3). *"...Lord, I believe, help my unbelief"* (Mark 9:24). *"...Depart from me, for I am a sinful man, O Lord"* (Luke 5:8).

Love, grace, mercy, goodness, and kindness create a light strong enough for people to see their own darkness and respond. People become aware of their sinfulness when grace is present. Goodness and kindness awaken people to see themselves outside of Christ and to move into repentance. People move out of their own darkness by stepping into the light of our fellowship with God. The world may not read the Scriptures, but they do read the Christians. God has written on our hearts the message of the Gospel. That message is our experience of Him in relationship and fellowship. What are people reading in us when they speak to us?

The Power of Goodness

The role of the Church is to establish the Kingdom. We do that by releasing all that Heaven has provided into the world. We create a glorious counter-culture that is all-powerful and all-consuming.

What if the biggest problem in any country is not lawlessness? What if it is not crime, poverty, adultery, abortion, drugs, or terrorism? What if the biggest problem is simply the lack of goodness? We overcome evil with good (see Rom. 12:21). So why is evil flourishing in our society? Possibly it is because the Church is so engaged in condemnation of sin and judgment on people that we are not employed in acts of goodness that render the enemy impotent. Instead we add to the environment that shields His presence and creates hardness of heart.

Sitting in a restaurant in Birmingham, UK, I was unaware that I was wearing my conference identification tag until the server told me. Her voice dripping with contempt, she told me in no uncertain terms what she felt about religion. Her anger and bitterness were evident. All this while she was pouring water! I had choices. Would I become annoyed, defensive, or offended? Would I leave the restaurant or feel persecuted?

The Kingdom allows for none of these. The Kingdom reveals Jesus and the nature of God. I wondered what He would say in my place and lifted my heart to Him to ask. I felt His compassion for her. I stepped into it, listening for His heartbeat. A telephone number came out of my heart into my conscious mind. I wrote it down.

"What is this Lord?" I asked internally. "She will find her son at this number," He breathed into my heart.

I could sense His joy for her. I gave her the number and the message. She looked at me, dumbfounded. Then her face hardened, and she sneered and went into the kitchen. She did not return, and we were given another server. Toward the end of the meal, she came back and stood by our table. Her face was different. There was a light, a peace, a weight lifted off of her soul.

Twelve years before, her husband, who had become a Christian a few years previously, divorced her and took their 8-year-old son. She had been struggling with depression and related illnesses. She lost the custody battle, and husband and son disappeared. The number I gave her was his cell phone. "How did you know?" she asked. I grinned at her. "I don't know anything" I said. "I just felt God's compassion for you. He is our Father, and He feels for us." A simple act of goodness opened her heart.

In a previous century, William Wilberforce (who helped to abolish the slave trade in the British Empire) started a movement that swept through the UK. It was called: "Let's make goodness fashionable." It changed the nation, redeemed society, and swept thousands of people into the Kingdom.

Flying to Singapore from London, I sat next to a Chinese woman who was clearly terrified of flying. During a particularly turbulent part of the flight, fear gripped her so badly that she was almost hysterical. She looked at me in horror, "Are we going to die?" I explained to her that she had the safest place on the plane, next to me. I was speaking at a conference the next day, and I knew what my assignment was from the Father for the event. So I was definitely not dying that day. I asked permission to pray for her, and she received the perfect love of God that casts out fear (see 1 John 4:18). A simple act of goodness opens the door of someone's heart.

No one is safe from a blessing. We have the whole world to victimize with the favor of God. Favor is the absolute, intentional bias of God toward His people. *"On earth as it is in Heaven"* was Jesus' greatest prayer (Matt. 6:10). *"As He is, so are we, in this world"* (1 John 4:17). We are walking in His footsteps. We have Christ within, the Spirit filling us, and the favor of the Father.

This is good news of great joy. The role of the Church is to release the presence of God and the purpose of the Kingdom. We are a reconciling, redemptive society that represents the glorious nature of God and the irresistible power of His Kingdom. We are engaged in displacement.

We do not rail against sin; we call down the grace of God. Where sin abounds, grace does *much more* abound (see Rom. 5:20). Where we see cities and communities overtaken by sin and wickedness, we do not proclaim judgment. The work of the Holy Spirit is to convict the world concerning judgment. He does that by informing the world that the devil has been judged on their behalf (see John 16:8-11). Our ambassadorial role is to bring freedom, to lead people out of their enslavement. It is for freedom that Christ has set us free (see Gal. 5:1). The devil has lost his power and is defeated by the blood and sacrifice of the Lord Jesus.

We go to places of iniquity to call down grace. Over every place where wickedness is present, grace is available in huge proportions. Drop a brick into a bowl of water and displacement occurs. Get enough churches in a location to access the Kingdom together and we can call down our corporate favor onto the community. Mercy triumphs. Goodness overcomes. Love covers. Grace abounds. Joy strengthens. Peace surpasses. Favor encompasses.

A Kingdom Approach to Life

The Kingdom of God is within us (see Luke 17:20-21). Jesus said this to the Pharisees. The Kingdom is everywhere and in all people. The law of creation is the law of the Kingdom. It was built at the foundation of the world and built into the structure of our very being. It's in our personality because it's in the universe around us. When we sin against God, we rebel against ourselves and the universe. When the prodigal came to his senses, it was to acknowledge to his father, *"I have sinned against heaven and before you, and I am no longer worthy to be called your son..."* (Luke 15:18-19).

Sin affects us in three places. First, it affects our experience of the Kingdom of Heaven in terms of our ascended lifestyle in Jesus. Second, it affects our relationship with the personal love of the Father. Third, it causes us to sin against ourselves because our identity as sons and daughters comes under threat.

The Kingdom of God is our home, our Canaan. We inherit the Kingdom from the Father. Also, the Kingdom comes upon us in the person of Jesus (see Luke 11:20). It is personalized to us as we receive Christ. As we are born again, we get to see the Kingdom around us, operating in all its fullness and glory (see John 3:3). We enter the Kingdom as an experience upon conversion (see Matt. 18:3). Indeed, the process of conversion includes a developing experience of Kingdom life. We develop our personal destiny in the light of God's universal destiny for humanity.

Our life is an extension of the Kingdom, and it empowers us to flow with God's universal Kingdom purpose. One person can change the universal destiny of a city, a nation, a people group by embracing the Kingdom on their behalf. I can adopt my whole neighborhood within the Kingdom that I represent in my relationship with God.

Walking around my old sub-division of around a hundred homes and being aware of the Kingdom both within and around me is lots of fun. There is favor over every household because the Kingdom is universally present and everyone has already been reconciled to God. As an ambassador of Christ, it is my role to work with the Holy Spirit to upgrade people from reconciliation (already bestowed by the Father) to redemption in Jesus by declaring and demonstrating the favor of God.

Prior to Calvary, Jesus preached the Kingdom as a present reality and demonstrated its power with signs following. Walking around my neighborhood with the Holy Spirit and discovering His presence and purpose for families is an enjoyable experience. I used to hate door-to-door work until I realized that the reason I received so much rejection was because my timing was wrong. I was not working in partnership with the Holy Spirit so I had not discerned which homes He was working in. When I began to ask the right questions, I started to pray over the homes that He indicated.

As a result, I showed up at those houses with a particular gift as an expression of the Kingdom. In the UK, at one house in my area, the Holy Spirit showed me that the guy who lived there was out of work, over 50, and desperate. When I prayed for him, the Holy Spirit gave me a particular piece of favor to bestow. When he opened the door, I had a specific gift to offer him that would introduce Jesus and the Gospel of the Kingdom.

Of course, there is always the initial awkwardness of invading someone's space uninvited. I try to keep it light, friendly, and short. I also have something written down on a nice card with my phone number. When their space is being invaded, some people don't hear too clearly, and it's good to hand them something to see.

In this man's case, I had a prophetic word that he would be in a job in the next few weeks. The Holy Spirit told him where the job could be found and how to access it. Initially he was fairly aggressive and suspicious, which is understandable.

"Hi," I said, "my name is Graham. I'm a Christian. I live down the street. I have been praying for your family and believe that God has a gift for you. He showed me that you need a job, and He wants you to have this one." It took around twenty seconds to say; then I handed him the card. He looked at me as if I was a freak (understandable) and read the card. In that city, the local newspaper has a job-finding supplement every Thursday evening. The card simply said: "page 45, 3rd column across, 2nd advertisement down, God is giving you this job."

He looked at it, looked at me, swore at me, called me a freak, and slammed the door in my face (understandable). The Kingdom is not a normal experience for most people, so it quite naturally feels a little odd. Later I discovered Kevin's story. He was working for a company and was recruited by another company, given a promotion and an upgrade in salary. His old company moved their premises, and the personnel files were destroyed by mistake. His new company lost a contract and laid-off hundreds of people, including Kevin.

Several years later, the first company was expanding, and Kevin's old job was available. They wanted to contact him, but they had no records, and he had moved. In the newspaper, page 45, column 3, 2nd job down was his old company's advertisement of his old job. Kevin had become depressed at so many job rejections that he had not bought the newspaper for six months.

He called the company and was hired over the phone! He then called me. We had coffee, and he began his journey into the Kingdom.

Apprehended by Goodness

Jesus was passing through Jericho when He saw Zacchaeus, a rich tax collector, up a tree (see Luke 19:1-10). This guy was notorious in the neighborhood for defrauding people. He was distrusted and disliked by everyone. The whole community would have loved to entertain Jesus at their home. They could possibly have dined out on the story for the next 12 months. But Jesus chose Zacchaeus, much to everyone's annoyance. He honored the one person in the district that was the least deserving.

While hurrying to catch up to Jesus, Zacchaeus came to a life decision. Half of his possessions he would give to the poor, and all those whom he had defrauded he would repay at 400 percent. Jesus never spoke about any of that. It was not a precondition of their fellowship. His goodness in honoring a man despised in his community was enough to overcome all of the avarice in that man's heart.

Can you imagine the scene the next day, after Jesus had moved on? There is a knock at your front door, and there stands a man you loathe, who has defrauded you of much-needed income. He looks agitated, unsure of himself, not like the crafty, conceited individual you are used to seeing. Nervously he hands you a money pouch; it's heavy. "I'm sorry, so sorry, for cheating you," he stammers, before turning and scurrying away.

"Who was that?" shouts your wife from the kitchen as you close the front door and enter the living room. "Zacchaeus," you reply, tipping the contents of the bag onto the table. "What did that little rat want?" she says, coming into the living room. She moves to your side, and you stand together staring at the heap of money on the table. It's four times the money that you lost. In tears, you embrace one another. Finally, your troubles are over. "What happened?" asks your wife tearfully, burrowing her head into your shoulder. "Jesus," you say. "It must have been Jesus."

Throughout the community, that same scene is being repeated. One man's goodness liberates the whole community. Favor comes upon everyone. It is the power of goodness to overcome.

Intercessors are a key part of the Gospel of the Kingdom. They band together in dark places and pray down the light, the grace, and the goodness of God. Displacement is a key element to warfare (see Luke 11:14-26).

In a postmodern world, the reception of truth has changed. The organ of receptivity used to be the ear. People came to hear and receive truth. In these different times, there are different perceptions of truth. Postmodern people say, "You have your truth; I have my truth. You respect my truth as I respect yours."

We live in a show-and-tell world where the organ of receptivity is the eye. People want to see God in action. They need Church to regain its supernatural ministry in the Kingdom. We are seeing a return to the book of Acts, a demonstration of power, theology in practice.

The Father is working, and we work with Him. We learn sensitivity to the Spirit as we are led by Him into divine encounters with people. We do only what the Father shows us to do, in the way that He wants it done. We live a celebratory lifestyle as much-loved children. We are caught up in the joyous, cheerful, loving nature of God. We receive His passion for people. We live our lives in dependence and wonder with a radiant idea of God and His Kingdom. We love favor, blessing, and intimacy. No one around us is safe from the goodness of God.

He involves us in His love, grace, mercy, and goodness. We travel with great news of great joy. Many Christians act like an undertaker at a birthday party. God loves to connect with people at any time. Sometimes His outrageous sense of fun makes our lives a little interesting.

Goodness Draws Them Near

Driving down a major freeway in England, I hit a traffic jam that crawled along at five miles an hour when it wasn't completely at a standstill. The guy in the huge car in the lane next to mine looked the epitome of a successful businessman—well-fed, well-scrubbed, well-dressed, chewing on a huge cigar, driving a car that cost as much as my house. I felt that small stirring of joy, which one of my previous mentors would have called the unction of the Spirit. I opened my heart to listen.

God told me that this man was driving to meet his lawyer to draw up the papers to sell the business he loved. Apparently he had a huge cash flow problem because he had numerous debtors who had not paid him for months. Cash flow exhausted, he was looking to liquidate his assets and avoid bankruptcy.

I felt the Father's promise to him was that his debtors would pay up in a matter of weeks and that he should not sell the business. God knew how much he loved it. I wrote down the promise. I wound down my window, leaned across, and rapped on his. When he opened it, I threw the folded piece of paper into his car. I don't know what he was thinking, but all kinds of thoughts were going through my head, most of them embarrassing!

Don read the paper and did a classic double take. The traffic began to move. "Next service area!" he shouted. Ten miles down the road, he confirmed the word of knowledge. He was not a believer but requested prayer. He called his lawyer and rearranged their meeting for a month later. He never made it. Money was repaid, and he stayed in business. The Kingdom had intervened, and the King had another joyful supplicant.

An Islamic shopkeeper, from whom I used to buy my daily newspaper, was having difficulties. It was just after 911 in America. Ali wanted to remodel his store but was worried that he would lose business if he closed for refurbishment. We had struck up an unlikely friendship over many months. A devout Muslim, he knew that I loved Jesus.

One day in an empty store, he confided to me his problem. "What would your best solution be?" I asked him. Pursing his lips, he finally said, "To be able to transfer my business to a nearby store so that I could carry on my business and watch over the development of this store. But that is impossible, so *Insh Allah* (as God wills it). It never occurred to him to ask God for help. Islam is largely a fatalistic religion where people passively accept life events and circumstances.

I knew that the Father wanted to be invested in Ali's situation. As I prayed, His will became clear. I wrote a crafted prayer for Ali in which he had permission to ask God for what he really wanted. We talked in his store. I prayed with him and gave him the crafted prayer for his business. He was intrigued about praying to Jesus but promised to do it. I left soon after for a month-long tour of America.

When I returned, I went to get my newspaper but found the store closed for remodeling. I heard a shout and saw Herdeep, Ali's wife, across the road in the doorway of a store. As I reached her, she led me in and there was Ali behind the counter serving. The place was full of people.

Ali saw me and shouted, "Brother, your God has answered our prayers!" We hugged and his family crowded around, touching me and calling out blessings. His whole family had prayed the prayer every day. Many of them took out pieces of paper where they had copied the prayer.

Door-to-door, between both establishments, was only 40 feet. Ali had a 90-day rental, which is unheard of in that community. The God of goodness got involved, establishing business as usual in the Kingdom.

No one does life like the Father. The God of gladness loves His world. His heart is open to the cries of people. He loves to deliver and empower. He seeks partners who will share His love and demonstrate His loving kindness. The enemy has lost the streets, and we own them as we step up into the Kingdom that is present. Jesus has triumphed, and mercy waits to fall on a world still being poisoned by sin and selfishness.

The world's problem is not the enemy. It is a Church unfamiliar with the Kingdom and unbelieving about the power of goodness. Our biggest obstacle to reformation is a Church that has no practical experience of being seated in heavenly places in Christ (see Eph. 2:6). Our theology espouses authority but does not practice it. We live below our privilege and are overruled by powers, principalities, and spiritual wickedness in high places (see Eph. 6:12-13).

The nature of God is the place where we recover our God-given right to rule and reign.

To me, the very least of all saints, this grace was given, to preach to the Gentiles the unfathomable riches of Christ, and to bring to light what is the administration of the mystery which for ages has been hidden in God who created all things; so that the manifold wisdom of God might now be made known through the church to the rulers and the authorities in the heavenly places.

This was in accordance with the eternal purpose which He carried out in Christ Jesus our Lord, in whom we have boldness and confident access through faith in Him (Ephesians 3:8-12 NASB).

NOTES AND APPLICATIONS

Chapter 7

WILLING TO LOSE

Steve Sjogren

IN HIGH SCHOOL, my friends and I spent many Sundays riding down Arizona's Salt River on inner tubes. Little did I realize that our version of fun was pretty dangerous.

Arizona is a seasonal state with many regions of weather that vary according to the rainfall or snowfall. In the spring, the melting of the mountain snow causes the Snake River to flood magnificently. Those who are up for an adventure float down the river on make-shift rafts or individual tubes to run the rapids. Depending upon the week, the water can be both cold and fast. I didn't realize it at first, but more than a few kids my age were drowning due to the combination of sun, fun, and beer. It's not good to combine the awesome power of nature with a laid-back attitude toward river danger. Someone is bound to get hurt.

It wasn't long before one of our friends was seriously hurt. Donnie nearly drowned when the undertow caught him, pinned him under a submerged tree limb, and kept him there until he shook loose. The buzz of beer and the daze from whacking his head didn't help matters.

I may be slow on the initial uptake, but I am not slow once the shot comes over the bow of my boat, so to speak. When danger comes close by, I am usually one of the first ones to pack up and hear my Mama calling me to come home.

The Big God Experience

Like me on the Snake River, outsiders to the Kingdom are looking for someone to rescue them from danger. In high school, we can run home to our parents. But when the troubles of adult life overtake us, where can we run? Have you spoken to any not-yet believers lately? They are looking desperately for the God of big wins. They are not looking for a feeble, miserly God who is barely making it, barely able to help His followers. They have an innate belief in a supernatural God who is in control of all things. I like to refer to this picture as "Big God."

I had my own definition of Big God etched onto my heart in the midst of a tremendously long and difficult physical ordeal a few years ago. Because of a medical mistake, I fell into a coma. After I was unconscious for a number of days, the medical personnel and my family began wondering if I would be normal after being out of commission for so long. My wife, Janie, was told that I would probably be verbal but that she should not get her hopes up too high. If I did get better, they said, it would probably not be a full recovery because of the lengthy time of low blood pressure that I had experienced.

When I was coming around, everyone gathered around the bed to hear the first words that I, a potentially brain-damaged person, would say. I remember the doctors saying my name over and over. "Steve, Steve—can you hear me?" It was kind of irritating to hear them saying this repeatedly, so I was ready to speak. "Can you hear us?" I shook my head to indicate "yes." "How do you feel?" I shook my head "no" to indicate that I felt bad. "Can you hear us, Steve?" they asked one more time.

This time I said the thing that was burning in my heart.

"BIG."

Coma Time

All I could think to say, regarding my ordeal, focused on my meditation over the past two weeks. The medical personnel had told Janie that they thought I was more or less sleeping during this time. Nothing could have been farther from the truth. I don't think I was unaware of a single moment during that entire time. For whatever reason, the medication that they gave me kept me wide awake. It was the most amazing time that I have ever had. I wasn't tired at the end of it. I spent my time, uninterrupted, in the presence of God. I focused completely on Him.

My family and friends were praying for my survival during this ordeal. That was a great thing to pray for. On the surface, my life was indeed on the line. I weathered through something only a handful of people can say they have experienced—a double aorta puncture and the complete depletion of their blood supply (it was necessary to refill my blood supply several times over during my time in the coma, but that part was not painful). Of the over 300,000 who have had this accident happen to them, only four have survived it as of this writing.

But the odds of surviving weren't my focus during the coma. Day after day, hour after hour, my time on the river of God's presence occupied my attention. In a way, the whole thing was a gift to me. On the physical level, it was unbearably painful. I explain this in great detail in my book, *The Day I Died*.[1] But when the dust settled, I found that the entire experience had been a priceless gift.

I have been ruminating on the love that I have been shown by God in this gift for years now. I was forced to slow down, to study the things that God made me for. Such a gift is rare. Considering the pace at which I had been living, I likely would have lived out my days at a breakneck pace with no capacity for realizing my calling in Jesus. I was moving so fast that I was unaware of the awe of God. Without awe, I never would have encountered His power.

Years after the accident, I am still recovering my physical agility, but I am alive and kicking. Much more importantly, I have grown in love with the slowing of life. I can now move through life with God and have a tremendously good time. God is not one to disappoint those who eagerly look for Him.

First Words

During most of the two weeks of my coma time, I meditated on one simple notion: God. For the first time, I had to lay motionless in a bed, unable to do anything but focus upon the Maker of all that is. I had studied about God for years as a pastor, but I had been so easily distracted for most of that time.

Now that I had awakened from the coma, I was being asked to say something—anything to give my family and doctors an indication that I was alive and well. All that I could say was the adjective that came into my mind that best described God at that moment. *He is, uh, BIG!* I said to the small group gathered around my bed, "Big, big, big, big."

The doctor didn't look very encouraged. My voice was raspy from the dryness of the medical equipment. It must have made for a sorry sound. The doctor leaned over to my wife to whisper something in her ear, something akin to, "This may be a long process. He may have lost more than we thought." She didn't look all that encouraged. And she wasn't smiling.

She was with the doctor as they leaned toward me. The repetitions of "big" hadn't gone over well with them. "Big what, Steve? What are you talking about when you say 'Big'?"

"God. Big God. Big God."

With that, I teared up. I was able to express my heart at last. I wanted to share the discovery of my two-week search after God. There it was. Just two words.

Ironically, as a pastor, I had previously given hundreds of messages focused on helping people find the reality of God's nature. Now I had come to the simplicity of who God is—His power, His presence—and it all came down to just two words. But those two words meant: He is many things, but above all else, perhaps God is BIG. God is Big, big, big. I couldn't believe the utter simplicity, compactness, and (at the same time) awesomeness of God in that statement. "Big God." That's who He is above all else.

Flight

On a recent flight, I sat next to an executive with a Fortune 100 Corporation, a cheery enough chap who happened to live in a city where a friend of mine had started a church. I had spoken there, so I was familiar with the city, and he was very familiar with my friend's church. When I mentioned it, he immediately perked up, saying that the place was well-known in the city.

"Everyone in the city knows those guys. It's just an unusual church—they love people there." I knew this church was known for its outreach to the downtrodden, forgotten, and addicted. Many who never went to church considered this their church though they never attended. Apparently my seat mate was one of that crowd. It was the church for many in the city—kind of a, "If I were to go to church, that's the place I'd call home...."

He felt he needed to correct my description though. "Your friend didn't start that church. You need to know that. In fact, I don't think any person started that church. You can't just start a church like that."

I wasn't sure where he was going. I knew the story. It was certain that my friend had started the church. I had been there a number of times, including once during the early days when the place had just a few dozen people. I was puzzled by his description.

He continued, "Those kinds of places have just always been in places like that. That's what I believe. You can't have a meeting of people and decide among a few people, 'Hey let's start a church' and pretty soon a church pops up. It doesn't work that way. Churches are the result of something far larger than that. That church taught me that lesson."

He wasn't trying to be profound. He was just speaking from his heart. As he shared with me, he got misty-eyed. He caught me off guard with his candor. I decided to not mess with the astonishing line he offered, and we moved on to another topic. He was so caught up in God's *presence.*

So what makes a guy like my seat mate carry on as he did? Why would he claim that churches like my friend's don't just start but that they are always there? He was referring to the presence of God that has been a large part of my friend's church.

Typically, when we refer to the hugeness of God, the conversation moves pretty quickly to this notion that God is so large that He is out of our control almost immediately. He is to be noticed, to be worshiped, to be loved, but for Him to be controlled in any sort of way is a joke.

What does it take to understand the presence of God? Perhaps it is even beyond us to understand much of the presence of God. But we can grow a step or two in that direction if we set our minds toward that end.

Cry of the Human Heart

The cry of all of our hearts is to discover the edges of the God who can do anything.

I raised all three of my children to experiment with this notion about God—that He is awesome and that He is worth getting to know more and more. I helped coax them into thinking that it was normal to devote Saturday mornings to caring for people in need. It is an awesome thing to spend time on a regular basis with those in physical need.

Why? Those in clear physical need have broken down their barriers to God. They don't need to be convinced that they have need of God. They walk in the daily awareness of that need.

They are the ones who Jesus called blessed: *"Blessed are the poor in spirit* [those who know their need]. *Theirs is the kingdom of God"* (Matt. 5:3 NASB). When we spend time with people who already realize that they are bankrupt at the physical realm, we tend to catch the overflow of their spiritual truthfulness.

At 10:30 A.M., for two hours each Saturday, I would take my kids out to care for people in need in various parts of the city where people in need lived. We would carry food and clothing to mostly single parent families toward the end of their food supply months, helping them to carry over from the 29th day to the 30th. (There are usually a couple of days of carry-over need in the calendar of all who receive government assistance. That was when we would show up with help.)

One Saturday, I was with my young daughter, Laura, and a couple of friends as we gave out bags of groceries door-to-door in a needy neighborhood.

One lady was stuck in a wheelchair and facing serious surgery. In fact, chances were that, if she wasn't able to move her leg to a certain degree, there would be an amputation the following week. The family had a seriousness about them when we showed up with groceries.

They were grateful, but they really wanted prayer. We prayed a simple prayer. We asked God to do what no person had been able to accomplish yet—to heal grandma's leg so that she could move it. At the end of the prayer, we said, "Be healed, leg." The lady said that she didn't feel much of anything. We prayed again with more vigor.

Sometimes it takes an active engagement of our prayers. I am fairly often a big chicken, truth be told. This time the line, "Leg, be healed," came out with faith. The lady said that she felt something kick in. Warmth was beginning to touch her leg from the top to bottom by her ankle. We thought, *Third time is a charm!* This time we internally prayed for help on the prayer. "Leg, be healed!" All three of us felt something almost as an impartation from God through us to that lady.

The lady's leg got hot that time. She felt like something was coursing through her. She started saying encouraging words and phrases like, "Wow," and "My oh my," and "That's what I'm talking about!" Just listening to her got me excited. I asked the obvious question. "So how do you feel, lady?"

"I feel great! I don't know what you all lit, but it's burning in my leg like crazy here. I could feel something moving down my leg to my ankle. This was the first time I felt anything in my leg for many months. I feel like a million bucks. Thank you, Lord! You know I haven't said or thought that in I don't know how long. Thank you, Lord!"

She looked like a completely different person compared to when we started to pray for her. Best of all, she lifted her leg up a bit and bent her ankle—it moved significantly. It was far more than the move the doctors were looking for in order to declare her OK the following week.

The family was ecstatic. To them, this was as big a moment—bigger than the Prize Patrol and Ed McMahon visiting them with the Grand Award of the season, letting loose the balloons in that little apartment. It was a gift from Jesus for them alone.

Regardless of the parameters, they realized that this was all arranged by God for them. This was the work of Big God on their behalf. Grandma may have lost her leg if something pretty significant hadn't happened that day. But now all had turned around. God's presence had shown up. God's power had been manifest.

Return Trip

A number of us came back to that neighborhood some months later. As we were going along, a girl in the apartments said, "You all look a little familiar. Were you here some months ago?" As we affirmed that, she asked if we happened to know who had prayed for the woman she referred to as the neighborhood "Granny." We said that we had.

She responded, "Granny has been through a lot in the past several months. She didn't need surgery after all. She has been in therapy. She got rid of the wheelchair after a few weeks of therapy. She has been telling everyone that she has had a change of heart—something about thinking differently and relying on God now. All I know is that she is walking—no need for a cane or anything. She was in that wheelchair for a long time and now—well, you can see for yourselves if you can find her. She is feeling pretty good, so you may have to hunt her down first. She gets around a fair bit."

I was dumbfounded. She had been on the verge of going down for the last time. But now—well you get the idea. It's simply amazing what can happen when God gets involved.

The Opposite of Fear

John tells us that God's perfect loves casts out fear (see 1 John 4:18). It's funny how we tend to think in dimensions and opposites. Most would vote to say that the opposite of love is hatred. Why? We tend to extend a rigorous, strong feeling in hopes of battling an opposing notion.

God realizes that life doesn't work that way. He understands that the enemy of our best is the leaking of that best effort, not the attacking of that effort. Love, in this case, is leaked by the little things that dribble it out of commission. Fear is the opposite of love because fear leaks love. Hate isn't the leaking of love. Hatred is on another track altogether.

Fear is the drain of the power of love. You and I have the presence of God's life dwelling in us as Jesus' followers. His presence is diminished when we give in to the itsy bitsy fears that nag at us in day-to-day life. Those are the fears that rob us of all life.

The enemy uses fear as a sneaky attack. It's so small that we don't see it coming. We often don't even count it as attack. It just seems like a little irritation. So we usually miss identifying fear as the deadly attack that it is.

Gamblers

Fear is our enemy because God builds His Kingdom using those who are willing to *risk* big for the things that excite Him. God does not require that we have our faith house in order before we are involved with His Kingdom. He is looking for people in process. But His Kingdom is arranged for those who are willing to continually say "yes" and who are willing to risk their lives for the great things of the Kingdom.

God wants people who are willing to lose all else for His Kingdom's purposes. He is looking for the "gamblers," the big-riskers. Hebrews 11, often called the "Hall of Faith," tells us of people who took, in faith, the little that they had and translated it into much—performing great acts for God—as they applied it by the power of faith that God supplies.

Some ask, "If faith is a gift of God (see Eph. 2:8), and if we have all been given a measure of faith from God (see Rom. 12:3), then why do we not all perform great exploits like the Hall of Faith folks?"

The variable, which we can control, is how willing we are to respond to the dare. Are we the daring people of God? Or are we people who live in fear that something out of our control might happen? Do we live in fear of loss? Or do we battle those fears?

We can simply walk away from fears, recognizing that they are just the lies that plagued us when we were living in the shadow of death, as David wrote (see Ps. 23:4).

God has arranged this life as a gigantic game of risk. But when we see God's bigness in our lives and His grace for every task, we then see that our "risk" is not risky at all compared to living apart from God. In fact, we will learn that life with God is no risk at all (though it often *feels* risky) because He is perfectly faithful.

Endnote

1. Steve Sjogren, *The Day I Died* (Ventura, CA: Regal Books, 2006).

NOTES AND APPLICATIONS

Chapter 8

PROPHETIC EVANGELISM: INTIMACY FOR POWER

Dr. Craig von Buseck

THERE WAS A DROUGHT IN THE LAND of Israel—a drought of the prophetic word of God. Prior to the arrival of John the Baptist, heralding the appearance of Jesus the Messiah, the prophetic word had not been heard for more than 400 years.

This prophetic drought brought with it the spiritual climate that produced the Pharisees and the Sadducees. It also brought about the religious intolerance that would exclude the Gentiles, isolating the Jews from the world that God had intended for them to reach.

For it was always God's intention that through Israel—both natural and spiritual—that all the nations of the earth would be blessed (see Gen. 22:18).

But the Jews had cut themselves off from the Gentiles, thinking that the call to be a holy people meant a call to be separated from the rest of the world. Jesus said this of His people, the Jews:

In their case the prophecy of Isaiah is being fulfilled, which says, "You will keep on hearing, but will not understand; you will keep on seeing, but will not perceive" (Matthew 13:14 NASB).

The spiritual wells of Israel had been backfilled with the sands of religious tradition and intolerance. And the prophetic voice of God was absent from the land.

And so it was, in this barren spiritual climate, that the Messiah came to rest at Jacob's well in Samaria after a long, hot journey. It was just about high noon, and Jesus was fatigued from the heat. Suddenly a woman appeared on the hazy horizon, walking toward Him carrying a large earthen pot.

It was an unusual time to draw water. The sun was high in the sky, scorching the Mediterranean countryside. The other women had drawn water early in the morning when it was cool. But this woman did not want to be at the well when the others were there. She had a past. She had a reputation. She was the topic of gossip and derision, and she knew it.

No, she didn't want to face the uncomfortable stares and the forced smiles of the other women. So she came at the hottest time of the day to the well to draw water for her household.

The woman saw Jesus sitting next to the well from afar and approached cautiously, curious to know who this stranger was. Jesus was alone, for His disciples had gone away into the city to buy food. He turned to her and initiated the conversation. "Give Me a drink."

The Samaritan woman immediately recognized the Galilean accent and was surprised that a Jew would speak to her, for they had no dealings with Samaritans. Her reply was both inquisitive and flirtatious, for she knew how to charm a man. She cocked her head and smiled slightly. "How is it that You, being a Jew, ask me for a drink since I am a Samaritan woman?"

Jesus was not moved by the flirting. He had spiritual business to do. Without hesitating, He answered, "If you knew the gift of

God, and who it is who says to you, 'Give Me a drink,' you would have asked Him, and He would have given you living water."

The woman was used to men playing word games. It was all a part of the now tiresome exchange that led to the counterfeit she had come to believe was love. She decided to play along, thinking that this was just another come-on from yet another stranger. With a playful note of sarcasm, she answered, "Sir, you have nothing to draw with and the well is deep. Where will you get this living water?"

She was tired of others making themselves to be better than her. She was tired of the pious airs put on by the women of the town with their own ghosts in the closet. She was sick of the looks of superiority from people all around her who would do all they could to put her in her place. And here was a Jew, someone from the same lineage as her people, the Samaritans, and yet carrying that same superior attitude—or so she thought.

The disdain bubbled up from within her, spewing forth in thinly veiled anger. "You are not greater than our father Jacob, are You, who gave us the well, and drank of it himself and his sons and his cattle?" *That's right, **our** father Jacob. You are no better than I am. We Samaritans descend from the same bloodline as you.*

Though the woman was tethered to her natural thoughts, formed by the culture and the times, Jesus was determined to set her free and bring her from the natural into the amazing world of the supernatural. Again, He did not respond to the racially charged question, but remained in the Spirit. "Everyone who drinks of this water will thirst again; but whoever drinks of the water that I will give him will never thirst; but the water that I will give him will become in him a well of water springing up to eternal life."

Now Jesus had her attention. He was offering two precious promises, though again she only grasped the natural interpretation. She wanted the equivalent of indoor plumbing—water that was available at the turn of a handle in the kitchen sink. But something else this Jewish man said jumped out at her: "eternal life." She wondered if salvation was even possible after the life of sin that she had lived. Though it was only a distant dream, she held on to the flickering hope that somehow she could come back into the faith and achieve eternal life.

Now she wanted what Jesus was offering, though she didn't quite know what it was. Still moored to the natural, she said to Him, "Sir, give me this water, so I will not be thirsty, nor come all the way here to draw."

Now Jesus stepped into the realm of the prophetic. Moving out in a word of knowledge, he said to her, "Go, call your husband and come here."

The woman was taken aback by the reply. Who was this stranger to probe into her personal life? It was a life that she did not want exposed—a life that she worked so hard to conceal. Her tone quickly became harsh, and she looked away from Jesus as she worked to untangle the rope at the well. She curtly answered, "I have no husband."

The tone of Jesus' reply again caught her off guard. It was not condemning. It was not sanctimonious. It was merely a gentle statement. "You have correctly said, 'I have no husband.'" The woman suddenly looked up from the rope and into Jesus' eyes. With compassion in His voice and love in His eyes for a lost soul who longed to be found, Jesus continued, "for you have had five husbands, and the one whom you now have is not your husband; this you have said truly."

The woman was perplexed by the truth of the words and the grace of the delivery. Stammering momentarily, she finally blurted out, "Sir, I-I-I perceive that you are a prophet."

Jesus remained silent and the truth of the moment became unbearable for the woman. Scrambling to take the spotlight off of her own sinful past, she tried again to move the conversation to the ethnic controversy. "Our fathers worshiped in this mountain, and you people say that in Jerusalem is the place where men ought to worship."

Jesus would not be roped into the natural conflict, but He again remained in the realm of the Spirit, saying to her, "Woman, believe Me, an hour is coming when neither in this mountain nor in Jerusalem will you worship the Father. You worship what you do not know; we worship what we know, for salvation is from the Jews. But an hour is coming, and now is, when the true worshipers will worship the Father in spirit and truth."

The hope that had been smoldering in the depths of her heart was suddenly fanned into flame with His words. Now the true faith of the woman emerged. She would not be kept from her salvation. From the depth of her heart, she proclaimed, "I know that Messiah is coming and when that One comes, He will declare all things to us."

Jesus knew that He had her heart. He looked the woman in the eyes and gently said to her, "I who speak to you am He."

Deep in her heart, she knew it was so. She smiled, holding her quivering hands up to her lips as in prayer. Her eyes filled and then overflowed with tears. She had no more words to say. Through the prophetic utterance of Jesus, she had been ushered from the natural into the supernatural, eternal world of wonder.

She backed away slowly, leaving her water pot, all the while smiling at Jesus through her tears. Then she turned and, with the joy of a prisoner who is suddenly and unexpectedly released, she ran into the city. Coming to a group of men, she cried out, "Come, see a man who told me all the things that I have done; this is not the Christ, is it?"

The woman ran from group to group throughout the town, gathering people to see this man who could be the Messiah. It didn't matter whether they had once condemned her. It didn't matter that they had shunned her. The prophetic word of the Lord had brought freedom to her, and now she wanted everyone to taste and see that the Lord is good!

And so, as a result of one simple prophetic word to the woman at the well, many of the Samaritans of that city believed in Jesus as the Messiah. (See John 4:5-32.)

One simple prophetic word.

The Power of the Prophetic

This is the evangelistic power of the prophetic word. It was prophetic evangelism like this that helped to build the early Church. And it has been prophetic evangelism, accompanied by signs, wonders, and miracles, that has propelled the Church forward around the world.

John Wimber called this "power evangelism," saying, "The clear proclamation of the finished work of Christ on the cross comes with a demonstration of God's power through signs and wonders. Power evangelism is a spontaneous, Spirit-inspired, empowered presentation of the Gospel."

Power evangelism takes the form of words of knowledge, healing, prophecy, and deliverance from demonic oppression. "In power evangelism," Wimber explained, "resistance to the Gospel is overcome by the demonstration of God's power, and receptivity to Christ's claims is usually very high."[1]

Thus, the New Testament believer should be eager to move in prophetic evangelism in order to effectively serve the Lord, to reach hurting people with the Gospel message, and to see the Great Commission—which is really the "Great Reminder"—fulfilled.

Eager to Prophesy

The apostle Paul urged believers to be zealous for the gifts of the Spirit—especially the gift of prophecy.

Pursue love, yet desire earnestly spiritual gifts, but especially that you may prophesy.... But one who prophesies speaks to men for edification and exhortation and consolation. One who speaks in a tongue edifies himself; but one who prophesies edifies the church. Now I wish that you all spoke in tongues, but even more that you would prophesy... (1 Corinthians 14:1, 3-5 NASB).

The prophetic has the unique ability to pierce the heart, break down defenses, and draw a person to salvation—just as it did with the Samaritan woman at the well.

Paul spoke of the special power that the prophetic word has for evangelism.

But if all of you are prophesying, and unbelievers or people who don't understand these things come into your meeting, they will be convicted of sin and judged by what you say. As they listen, their secret thoughts will be exposed, and they will fall to their knees and worship God, declaring, "God is truly here among you" (1 Corinthians 14:24-25 NLT).

Through one prophetic word, the heart of the Samaritan woman was melted, bringing her and her entire town to salvation. So the prophetic word spoken in season to an unbeliever can cause them to fall to their knees and declare that "God is in your midst."

Mark Stibbe writes that prophetic words "...can have a potent effect on unbelievers. For them it is like a piercing spotlight from heaven being shone into the darkness of their lives. This in return results in the disclosure of and exposure of who they are."

"When prophetic words hit the mark," Stibbe explains, "they function like the call of God to Adam and Eve in the garden. Unbelievers experience a profound sense of conviction. Like Adam and Eve after the Fall, they feel naked and ashamed and long to get right with God."[2]

That is why Paul gave us two admonitions regarding spiritual gifts:

But earnestly desire the best gifts (1 Corinthians 12:31a).

Wherefore, brethren, covet to prophesy, and forbid not to speak with tongues (1 Corinthians 14:39 KJV).

A study of the Greek New Testament shows that the only divine attributes that we are told to covet are the gifts of the Spirit. The phrase "covet earnestly" is from the Greek word *zeloo*, which means to have great desire for, to be jealous over, and to be zealously affected by. It means fervency of mind, or an emotional jealousy, as a husband would have toward his wife.

Paul said that any believer can prophecy as the Spirit gives them opportunity.

*For **you can all prophesy** one by one, that all may learn and all may be encouraged. And the spirits of the prophets are subject to the prophets* (1 Corinthians 14:31-32).

The gifts, or manifestations of the Spirit, are available to every believer.

*But the manifestation of the Spirit is given to **each one for the profit of all*** (1 Corinthians 12:7).

The wonderful promise from God through the prophet Joel is that, in the end times, the Spirit of the Lord will be poured out on all flesh—and all means *all*. Peter quoted this passage on the day of Pentecost:

*"And it shall be in the last days," God says, "that I will pour forth of My Spirit on all mankind; and **your sons and your daughters shall prophesy,** and your young men shall see visions, and your old men shall dream dreams; even on my bond-slaves, both men and women, I will in those days pour forth of My Spirit and **they shall prophesy"** (Acts 2:17-18 NASB).*

It doesn't matter if you are male or female, rich or poor, young or old—the Spirit of the Lord has been poured out, and you can prophecy! You don't even need to have the gift of prophecy or function in the office of the prophet. If you are a son or a daughter of God, you can receive and give prophetic words as the Spirit leads.

Prophetic evangelism, along with the other manifestations of the Holy Spirit, is available to the New Testament believer on an "as needed" basis. The only limit to moving in prophetic evangelism is our own faith.

*Since we have gifts that differ according to the grace given to us, each of us is to exercise them accordingly: if prophecy, **according to the proportion of his faith*** (Romans 12:6 NASB).

You might say, "Well, I don't have enough faith to prophesy." But if you are a born-again believer, you had enough faith for the greatest miracle of all, everlasting life. So if you had enough faith to be saved, I have good news for you, you have enough faith to move in prophetic evangelism!

The New Testament believer is to be zealous to move in the gifts of the Spirit for the purpose of being a witness to unbelievers and a minister of reconciliation. Because, in the end, that's what it's all about, being salt and light to lost and hurting people, just like the Samaritan woman.

The Ministry of Reconciliation

Just as Jesus had compassion on this woman who was an outcast from her community and brought the prophetic word that changed her world, so too He has compassion on all who are lost. He wants a family. His heart is for reconciliation.

And He has entrusted us with this same ministry of reconciliation.

*Now all things are of God, who has reconciled us to Himself through Jesus Christ, and has **given us the ministry of reconciliation**, that is, that God was in Christ reconciling the world to Himself, not imputing their trespasses to them, and has **committed to us the word of reconciliation**. Now then, we are ambassadors for Christ, as though God were pleading through us: we implore you on Christ's behalf, be reconciled to God* (2 Corinthians 5:18-20).

Once we come into the family of God, our Heavenly Father calls us to work in tandem with His Spirit to be ministers of reconciliation and ambassadors to those who are without God and without hope in the world.

Though they are a tremendous blessing to believers, the gifts of the Spirit are primarily given to empower us to be a witness to the lost. And the prophetic word is one of the most powerful evangelistic tools available to the New Testament Christian.

The first commandment of the risen Christ was for the disciples to return to Jerusalem to wait for the promised Holy Spirit so that they would be empowered to be witnesses.

But you will receive power when the Holy Spirit comes upon you. And you will be My witnesses, telling people about Me everywhere—in Jerusalem, throughout Judea, in Samaria, and to the ends of the earth (Acts 1:8 NLT).

The Holy Spirit is given to empower us to tell people everywhere that God is love and that He sent His Son into the world to make that love known. We see the love of the Father in Jesus. The world sees the love of the Father through our Spirit-empowered witness.

I was once invited to speak in a series of prophetic meetings across the state of Maine with Christian International's Network of Churches. We were ministering one afternoon in a church in Bangor, Maine. A young woman walked in about half-way through the service, and as soon as she entered the church, it was as if the Holy Spirit shined a spotlight on her, and He began revealing things to me concerning recent events in her life.

When the opportunity arose, I asked the young lady if I could pray for her. She rose and walked out into the aisle. I laid my hand on her shoulder and began to prophecy over her, describing what I was seeing in my spirit.

"I saw you sitting in your room, and you had the means and the will to take your own life," I began. Immediately she burst forth with tears. I continued, "But God sent someone to find you before you could go through with it. It was as if you were all alone and God took you and placed you into a family. He made sure your spiritual mother was there to care for you and get you the help you needed."

At that moment, a middle-aged woman who had been sitting next to her stood and embraced her. Both of them stood hugging each other in the aisle as I concluded. "She was able to bring you to a place where you received comfort and healing. And now that God has rescued you, He's calling you to be a part of His family."

I asked the young woman if she would like to make Jesus her Lord and Savior. As tears streamed down her face, she nodded yes, and we prayed a prayer of salvation as the other woman held her tight. After they sat down, the pastor asked if he could speak to me in the hall as one of the other ministers prophesied to someone else.

Out in the hallway, the pastor told me that the young lady had come to the church service directly from the hospital. She had been admitted just days before after attempting suicide. She was found by the middle-aged woman who had taken her into her home. As he conveyed these things, both of our eyes glistened with tears of joy at the new birth brought forth as a result of this prophetic word.

"Engage"

I was in a hurry one Saturday to return my rented videos to the library. But try as I might to get away from a leadership meeting at our church, I kept getting delayed by people wanting to talk. I arrived at the library just minutes before it closed, my mind distracted with the "to do" list for a busy Saturday as I waited in line to return my videos.

Suddenly, behind me in line, a young man in his early 20s started complaining loudly about the injustices of corporate America. I thought it a bit odd that a college-aged kid would be talking loudly to himself in the library about the ills of society. To be honest, I was a little annoyed by it.

Then God spoke to my heart. He said one word: "Engage."

I had to repent.

I turned to the young man and engaged him in conversation. "You know, that is true in some cases. There is a lot of greed and corruption in the corporate world. But not everyone is like that," I explained. "There are some people who work in the business world to help people and society."

"Shhhh," the librarian hushed us in typical librarian fashion.

"Why don't we meet out in front of the library after you return your books," I whispered, trying to be a good witness both to the young man and the librarian.

After a few minutes, we met in front of the library and started talking about good and evil and man's sinful nature. I explained that, as a result of the Fall, the heart of man was full of sin and selfishness. Every person on earth is in need of a Savior. The young man was extremely receptive to the Gospel message and, within only a few minutes, he expressed willingness to pray a prayer of salvation.

While we were still praying together, my son came bursting out of the library, all excited because our good friend was inside. This friend was the same age as this young man and was totally sold out to Jesus. I told my son to rush back into the library and tell him to come outside immediately.

My radical-for-Jesus friend came out just as I was finishing praying with the young man. "Dude, how are you doing?" my friend asked him, giving him a quick hug. As it turned out, my friend had been witnessing to this young man for months but had not led him in a prayer of salvation. The two young men exchanged phone numbers and my friend invited him to come and join their college-age fellowship group.

And all of this happened as a result of being sensitive to a single prophetic word—engage.

One Simple Prophetic Word

Che Ahn tells the story of how he was part of a ministry out-reach on a college campus when he observed a woman coming out of the student union building. Immediately the Lord gave him a word of knowledge that the girl was pregnant and considering an abortion.

He told me, in fact, this would be her second abortion. I quickly prayed and asked God for wisdom and grace in approaching her. Then I walked up and greeted her with kindness and explained that I was a pastor. "Please don't be offended, but I sensed God telling me that you are pregnant. God loves you, and He knows you are considering an abortion. In fact, this is your second time."

The young woman started crying and asked Che how he could possibly know these things. She said she had not even told her boyfriend. "Because God gave me the supernatural insight, I was able to share about God's love and salvation and His plans for her. In the end...both she and her boyfriend received Jesus."[3]

The two eventually became campus ministry leaders—all because of one simple prophetic word.

The Key of David: Intimacy Brings Power

So how does one flow dynamically in prophetic evangelism? The Bible makes it clear—and I have also found it to be true in my experience—that the Spirit of God moves powerfully in our lives when we spend time in the presence of the Lord.

We see an important example of this in the Old Testament Tabernacle of David. It is significant that, as King David brought the Ark of the Covenant into the Tabernacle, the spirit of prophecy filled the place and he declared:

...Let them say among the nations, "The Lord reigns" (1 Chronicles 16:31 NASB).

This prophecy confirmed the covenantal promise of God to Abraham, Isaac, and Jacob that, through Israel, all the nations of the earth would be blessed (see Gen. 22:18). The Church needs to understand that we, as spiritual Israel, are called to be a blessing to all the nations. And in order to flow powerfully in the prophetic, we also need to have a proper understanding of the Tabernacle of David and its significance to believers today.

David longed for the presence of the Lord so he brought the Ark of the Covenant into the tabernacle that he had erected in Jerusalem. When Asaph and his team of musicians ministered in the presence of the Lord before the Ark of the Covenant, it stirred up the prophetic voice of the Lord.

God inhabits the praises of His people (see Ps. 22:3). As Asaph led the people of God in worship around the Ark of the Covenant, the Tabernacle was filled with God's manifest presence. God is love, and love communicates. As they stood worshiping in His presence, God began to communicate. Many of the Psalms we have today come from this time of God's people seeking intimacy with Him in worship.

The Tabernacle of David is a type that foreshadows the life in the Spirit of the New Testament believer. Because of the grace of God, we are able to come boldly into His presence in worship and prayer, and as we do, God inhabits our praises. Because God is love, He communicates, speaking both to us and prophetically through us.

In order to be effective in prophetic evangelism, we must seek intimacy in the presence of the Lord. This, I believe, is the key of David.

The presence of God remained in the Tabernacle of David until the Ark of the Covenant was moved into the Temple of Solomon, where it was once again placed behind the veil in the

Holy of Holies. It remained behind the veil under the Law of Moses. Thus man was once again separated from the presence of God.

It was only after Jesus' sacrifice on the cross that the veil of the temple was torn open, once again giving mankind access to the presence of God (see Matt. 27:51).

We don't hear of the Tabernacle of David again until the book of Acts, when the Gospel suddenly spills over from the primarily Jewish early Church to the Gentiles through Peter, Paul, Barnabas, and others. This caused a great uproar among some of the Jewish believers, who insisted that the new Gentile converts follow the Law of Moses.

In Acts 15:6, Luke tells us that *"the apostles and the elders came together to look into this matter."* This was a critical test for the early Church. Luke wrote:

> *After there had been much debate, Peter stood up and said to them, "Brethren, you know that in the early days God made a choice among you, that by my mouth the Gentiles would hear the word of the Gospel and believe. And God, who knows the heart, testified to them giving them the Holy Spirit, just as He also did to us; and He made no distinction between us and them, cleansing their hearts by faith. Now therefore why do you put God to the test by placing upon the neck of the disciples a yoke which neither our fathers nor we have been able to bear? But we believe that we are saved through the grace of the Lord Jesus, in the same way as they also are"* (Acts 15:7-11 NASB).

Luke tells us that after Peter, Paul, and Barnabas shared the news of how God was doing signs, wonders, and miracles as a witness to the Gentiles through their ministries. James, the senior elder in Jerusalem, stood and made this important declaration:

*Simeon has related how God first concerned Himself about tak-ing from among the Gentiles a people for His name. With this the words of the Prophets agree, just as it is written, "After these things I will return, and **I will rebuild the Tabernacle of David which has fallen,** and I will rebuild its ruins, and I will restore it, so that **the rest of mankind** may seek the Lord, and **all the Gentiles who are called by my name,**" says the Lord, who makes these things known from long ago (Acts 15:14-18 NASB).*

It is vital that the Church make the connection here. The con-troversy at hand was about whether the Gentiles should be forced to follow the Law of Moses. Of all the Old Testament, James chose to quote what is seemingly an obscure passage from the prophet Amos. It was in the Tabernacle of David that God allowed wor-shipers into His very presence. We have to marvel at this remarkable suspension of the restriction under the Law of Moses that had kept man out of the presence of the Lord. God honored the faith and love of David, and as He did with Abraham, by His grace, He cred-ited it to him as righteousness and allowed the people of God into His very presence.

This was an unprecedented and never repeated act of God under the Old Covenant, and it pointed to how believers would relate to God under the New Covenant. In Christ we have access to the presence of God as a result of our salvation, which is secured by grace through faith. And just as He did in the Tabernacle of David, when we worship in His presence, God inhabits our praises and empowers us to be His witnesses in the earth.

Intimacy for Miracles

It is in the intimate presence of God that we are filled with His Spirit and empowered in the prophetic. If we want to move powerfully in the prophetic and in signs, wonders, and miracles for evangelism, we must spend time communing with God in His presence.

The prophet Amos declares that, when the Tabernacle of David was rebuilt, *the rest of mankind* would seek the Lord, and *all the Gentiles* who are called by God's name (see Amos 9:11-12). It is important for us to understand that, because of the shed blood of Jesus, the Tabernacle of David has been rebuilt for the New Testament believer. As we come to salvation, we have access to the presence of God, just as David and Asaph did.

When we spend time in the presence of God, He inhabits our praises, fills us with His Holy Spirit and power, and then speaks both to us and through us in prophetic utterances. With this infilling in the presence of the Lord, we are then empowered to take the Gospel to hurting people everywhere with signs, wonders, and miracles following the preaching of God's Word.

Jesus said that He is the vine and that we are branches; apart from Him we can do nothing (see John 15:5). We have the call of God to take the Gospel to every person on the earth—the "Great Reminder." We have God's promise that He has poured out His Spirit on all flesh and that we may all prophesy as the Spirit gives us the opportunity. So as we abide in the vine, He supplies the life and power to bear fruit in our lives and ministries.

Jesus went on to say, *"If you abide in Me, and My words abide in you, ask whatever you wish, and it will be done for you. My Father is glorified by this, that you bear much fruit, and so prove to be My disciples"* (John 15:7-8 NASB).

It is important to understand that this is a conditional promise—like the old if/then statements in computer programming. Jesus said that *if* you abide in Him *then* you will bear much fruit.

Because of the sacrifice of Jesus on the cross, there is no longer a spiritual drought on the earth. Instead there is now a growing flood of the prophetic word as individual believers allow the rivers of living water to bubble up from within them and to overflow to lost and thirsty souls—just like the hurting woman at that ancient Samaritan well who received the living water to never thirst again.

This is the key of David; intimacy with God fills us with power to move in prophetic evangelism as His witnesses in the earth. God wants a family, and there are still so many who need to hear that the Father loves them. So get into His presence—and then get out onto the streets!

Endnotes

1. John Wimber and Kevin Springer, *Power Evangelism* (San Francisco, CA: Harper San Francisco, 1992), 78-79.

2. Mark Stibbe, *Prophetic Evangelism* (Authentic Media, 2004), 80-81.

3. Che Ahn, *Fire Evangelism* (Grand Rapids, MI: Chosen Books, 2006), 168-169.

NOTES AND APPLICATIONS

Chapter 9

THE POWER OF NAMELESS
AND FACELESS PEOPLE

Wolfgang Simson

MY FRIEND, TONY COLLIS, is a well-known evangelist in New Zealand, and he currently pastors an Assemblies of God church in his country. Tony and his wife, Lynette, have a long-standing passion for the Church to return to its original roots, and they have been developing a small network of what they calls "micros"— small, organic communities or house churches.

Teaching about organic, community-oriented church in New Zealand, Tony told us, has not always been easy: "People seem reluctant to change, and feel very secure in the way they are doing church."[1] But the moment Tony took the very same message *abroad*, to a country outside of the Western world and culture, he was able to see how explosive his own message and conviction actually was. Here is Tony's report:

In January 2004, I was approached by a Christian leader from Myanmar—the former Burma—to come to his country and help him train church planters. He commented that it has taken him 26 years to plant 12 churches, and he did not want to take another 26 years to plant another 12 churches…could I help! He had read an article I had written on House Churches here in New Zealand, and he felt that such a form of church would work well in his country. His country has 50 million people, most of whom are Buddhist.

In January 2005, my wife and I flew to the capital of that country to train the first batch of church planters. In the following three months, the movement grew to 10 churches. In April, we encouraged and trained the same church planters, and the movement grew to 90 house churches in three months with an average attendance of five. In September, I visited again, and the house churches grew in strength to about 35 per house church. By the end of the year, 120 house churches were underway. In March 2006, I visited the country again to find 150 house churches. By then, they had a goal to see 500 house churches by the end of 2006. In early October, the movement had exceeded all expectations and had grown to over 1,000 house churches, now scattered all over the nation. I was in the country again at the beginning of November 2006, and they now have a vision to see 10,000 house churches as their next goal. An indigenous apostolic team is developing, and they are seeing apostolic fruit and effectiveness. While I was there, I heard the following testimonies.

Death and Back

One young church planter had started a house church in a small Buddhist village. The Buddhist monk was angry with the young evangelist and verbally attacked him in public. He then directed the young man to follow him to a cave on the outskirts of the village. Inside the dark cave, the Buddhist monk instructed the church planter to hold onto a small "glowing" stone. The monk began to call upon evil spirits to kill the young man, and as he did, his eyes glowed. Nothing happened to the church planter. Again the Buddhist monk called upon the evil spirits to kill the Christian. Again nothing happened. Third time the monk called upon evil spirits to kill off the church planter, and yet again, nothing happened to him, but rather the Buddhist monk fell to the ground dead. After a while, it dawned on the evangelist that if he left the cave alone, the people would think that he had killed the monk. Afraid of the consequences of leaving the cave alone, the man "resurrected" the monk, and they walked out together. As soon as they were both back in the village, the monk declared that the evangelist's God was stronger than his and that he was now going to become a Christian. The whole village came to Christ.

Take Your Beds and Walk

During a Church Planting conference in October 2006, one of the evangelists was asked to go to the hospital to pray for a friend's ill husband. He asked six of his fellow church planters to go with him. We prayed for the team before they left. When the seven arrived they stood outside the hospital and began to pray against the demonic spirits that were inside the compound. The guards watched with interest as they prayed fervently outside the gate. After a while they approached the door of the hospital. No visitors from other countries are allowed to look at the conditions of the hospital, so the entrance is guarded. These same guards require money from the local visitors, and these evangelists had none. As the evangelists approached, one of the guards extended his hand looking for some money. One evangelist laid hands on the guard and the soldier froze. He could not move, face and body locked into position. The rest of the Christians strolled in unhindered by the rest of the guards. They started to pray against all the spirits of sickness and disease in the hospital as they made their way to the room where the friend's ill husband was supposed to be. They found out that he had already returned home, so they decided that they would not waste the trip and started to pray for the sick. "Out…out…out" they demanded of the spirits of infirmity. One by one, people were healed. "Take up your bed and walk," commanded the evangelists. As each person had brought his own bedding, the healed did indeed gather up their bed stuff and left the hospital. Ten people were instantly healed and left the hospital before the team left. Doctors, nurses, family members, and the infirmed looked on with startled amazement. Others were prayed for and some came to Christ. The evangelists said that they had one more day left at the conference and that the people could ring them at a certain hotel tomorrow to inform them of other things that would happen as a result of their prayers. The next day, as we were hearing the story from the team of seven, the phone rang and more testimonies were given. The whole church planting group was inspired to step out with greater boldness.[2]

Loyal Obedience

These stories are powerful proof of God's continuing use of signs and wonders today. But let us step back a bit from these stories and look at some important Kingdom principles. Stories and experiences are one thing; biblical, objective truth is another. Personally, I decided to remain tethered to the pole of biblical revelation with all my life and to rate and observe any experience, no matter how exciting, as secondary, judged and weighed by biblical truth. Might is not right—God is right.

If we pose the question: "Why are there so few signs, wonders, and miracles happening in the Church of the cultural West in our days?" we will hear some standard answers.

Many in the non-charismatic segment of Evangelicals say that signs and wonders are not for today but that they served as an endorsement for the Gospel when it was first preached. A small group even goes so far as to say that, since the arrival of the biblical canon, all wonders are false, basically devilish, and empowered by hell itself. The charismatic and Pentecostal block says that we lack anointing and charisma and, therefore, need to ask for more, drink more, soak more, take in more. The faith movement says that we don't have enough faith. Most traditional churches believe that spiritual power is only for the clergy, for a select few.

In the same way that the diagnosis of a doctor defines the method of therapy, our analysis of the core problem will define our path to a solution. As a close observer of the phenomenon of explosive church multiplication around the world (did you know that around one million new house churches have been planted just in the last 10 years?), I have come to believe that the single most outstanding factor defining true and authentic spiritual power is *loving obedience to our King, Jesus.* Let me explain.[3]

Savior and King

Many Christians know Jesus as their savior; but a precious few actually allow Him to be the active and factual King of their lives. For most, Jesus is allowed to handle the salvation part, which many end up consuming and remembering in religious services and programs on a weekly basis.

But in the areas of sex, money, power, and church, in regards to life itself, they are practicing Amalekites. That terrible tribe harassed the Israelites in Old Testament times, and their name literally means "those who have no king." In these areas untouched by the Lordship of Christ, individual or corporate egoism, tradition, convenience, money, and personal desires, like safety-first, Middle Class values or a "Republican" mindset, dominate their lives.

Before you become too offended, let me explain that before *Republican* referred to a political party, it meant simply someone who believed in a republic form of government, as opposed to a *monarchy*. Many have become spiritual Republicans—they say, sing, and preach "Lord, Lord"—but they do not do as the King says (see Matt. 7:21).

The core DNA of Western culture has been so deeply molded by individualism, splendid isolation, and celebrations of our declaration of independence (both from God and from each other), that many have practically rejected each and any authority as inherently evil, as part of a bad "Big Brother" system that is trying to control and manipulate us.

And so we have become rebels. We have rejected not only the manipulative rulers, but also God's gentle rule. Because we have had many rulers, we have, in order to protect ourselves from more hurt, rejected God's offer to "rule under," His offer of Lordship, like a towel-bearing servant kneeling in front of us offering to wash our feet.

When we reject His humble leadership, we have silently joined that ancient and mad crowd cheering the verdict of Jesus before Pilate, screaming, *"We have no King but Caesar"* (see John 19:15) or the democratic and disobedient citizens who decided, *"We will not have this man to reign over us"* (see Luke 19:14).

Kneeling for the Blessing

Remember *fussball*, the most popular game on the planet? Soccer can be played officially—on clearly designated football fields with the FIFA rules in operation: 22 players, a referee, and goals that count. Or it can be played unofficially, outside the stadiums, on the parking lot, on the beach, or, as my sons do, when Mom isn't looking, in the kitchen. Both forms of the game are fun and exciting, but only one version counts.

Imagine a soccer field with four clearly designated lines that have names: sex, money, power, and religion. It is possible to play inside the field, according to the rules, obeying the norms and principles of the Kingdom, and to receive God's blessing.

But it is also possible to play offside, or even outside the legal framework of God. God would still love those illegal players and shower them (as it is His nature) with gifts of grace. But there is one thing that He will not give to them because He is bound to His own word; He cannot give them His blessing (see Deut. 28). Love and grace are completely unconditional; blessing is absolutely not. It is conditional, hinging entirely on God's big *if*: "If you obey my commands, if you obey my rules, if you walk in my paths, I will bless you."

How many people, who call themselves followers of God, are found playing outside of the Kingdom, the governmental framework of God, because they neither respect nor obey His official rules? We can recognize them quickly by an absence of blessing— by an evidence of no fruit that lasts, no multiplication, and no world impact (see Gen. 1:22,28).

When we receive God's blessing, obeying the rules and respecting God's blueprints for life, church, sex, money, and power, we see fruitfulness, multiplication, and rapid world impact—a movement of authentic, divine power. But this will happen only if we are not only loved and graced—but also blessed. And the blessing (the Hebrew word for blessing, *barakah*, means "knee") of the King requires that we are the kneeling subjects of the King.

Kneeling for Love

Why would anyone kneel in front of a king, voluntarily, freely, of his own choice, without being forced with a gun to his head? The answer is as simple as it is powerful: *love!* God loves us; we are invited to love Him back. We then fall hopelessly and madly in love with the family of the King, *our* new family, with *one another*. And then together we love the world, in self-sacrificial service, and do anything that it takes to introduce them to our King.

Whoever finds the King becomes His legal subject. Such a person vows to respect the King, His values and principles—the kind of justice that is valid before Him, His righteousness, and His Kingdom law—as top priority in life (see Matt. 6:33). Nothing can compete with the role that Jesus the King now plays in a new royal subject's life. And in a world where everyone screams for our loyalty—patriotism, religion, tradition, clans, money, supermarkets, power, fun, political doctrines, tithe-collecting churches, systems and gurus of all kinds—a person that is loyal to Jesus as King sticks out like a fish swimming against the tide.

Licensed for Power

Such a loyalty, a tested and proven loyalty, leads to *legitimacy*. Loyalty that does not stand up when challenged is cheap. Nobody gives a drivers license to a 15-year-old simply because he can drive a car really fast. The teenager has to demonstrate that he can handle the car and the traffic well and, even more, that he knows the traffic rules and actually abides by them. In Europe, driving licenses are issued only when one is 18. Prior to 18, the teenager had the ability, the *power*, to drive a car, but now he has the *license* to exercise this power and ability in an official, legal, recognized way.

The legitimacy of our loyalty is demonstrated in practical matters—like our sexuality. Sexual urges do not indicate that a person is ready or able to participate in disciplined and responsible sex that is not selfish and destructive. We need a "driver's license" for sex as well—marriage. Sex without a license trespasses God's creational order and borders, hurting blossoming life and demanding a horrendous price.

The same is true for *charismata*, the charismatic gifts of God, which are given to every child of God through the Holy Spirit. Charisma requires character, and truly precious gifts must be handled properly. The more powerful the gift that God gives us, the more maturity we will need in order to be good stewards of God's grace and to use His gifts according to His directives (which is the only way to avoid an unhealthy disaster).

Power (*dynamis* in Greek) in God's Kingdom is not just ability (*charisma*) to actually do something ("I can heal, therefore I heal; I can evangelize, therefore I evangelize"). Rather, Kingdom power is official power (*exousia*), legitimate power, power that is bound to the King, aligned to his Kingdom and, therefore, licensed and endorsed power.

Mere abilities, naively exercised without official license and endorsement, quickly become the foundation of misused, assumed power. Such usurped power inevitably leads to the establishment of self-centered, human empires because those quick to grab power

169

don't care for His Kingdom law. Such power, applied in ignorance, or even in defiance of God's rule, and dismissive about the directives of the King, is essentially theft. It is not backed by God.

Jesus' Loyalty

Even Jesus had to prove His loyalty to God. When He, *"being filled with the Holy Spirit, ...was led by the Spirit into the wilderness"* (Luke 4:1), He was challenged by Lucifer in three crucial tests. Why did Jesus pass all those tests? He did not argue, act in His own best interests, or use His ability (power) just because He had it at His fingertips.

He demonstrated a much more powerful truth: that He was *under orders*. Thus He referred back again and again to the law that was above Him: *"It is written"* (see Luke 4:4,8,12). Jesus proclaimed that He, unlike satan, was still voluntarily bound by God's Word. He was the intentional subject of an objective code that God had established, and therefore, Jesus could not and would not act in His own best interest, purely selfish and subjectively concerned with "what's in it for me." He demonstrated both to God and the devil the extent of His coming obedience: *"Not as I will, but as You will"* (see Matt. 26:39). This totally robbed the devil of any chance to handle Jesus.

But this is only one part of the story: before His Father in Heaven, Jesus had just passed the tests of His loyalty. Thus, He was handed the license and given the official nod to—from then on—use His charismatic gifts, His God-given powers, in an authorized and official way. Jesus returned from the desert as someone given *exousia*, authorized power, to perform *dynamis*, powerful signs and wonders. The desert was His graduation.

From then on, He was not only full of the Holy Spirit (full of abilities and possibilities), but He had also been given official license to use these abilities in accordance and in personal synchronization with His Father on a day-to-day basis (see John 5:19-20; 8:38). Does it not strike you that this moment is exactly the time when the ministry of Jesus was transformed, the power was "switched on," and literally the supernatural sparks flew?

Legitimate?

If Jesus needed such a legitimization of His own loyalty as the Son of God, will we be able to do without? The problem in the amazing power crisis of great segments of Christianity is not a lack of the power of the Holy Spirit or a lack of gifts, but a lack of authentication, of license that has to do with our shortcoming in legal Kingdom existence.

What does this mean? When we believe we can *play* church or ministry any way we want it (which is improper in the Kingdom), when we are not apostolic in the biblical sense (being sent forth by God, not sending out ourselves), when our motives are driven by anything other than our loving obedience to the King (wishing to do as He pleases), then the King will not command His presence.

He will always love us and grace us, but because He is bound to His own word, He will not bless us (see Deut. 28). He will not regularly confirm His word with signs and wonders (see Mark 16:20) because we are not really His authentic subjects, legitimately bound to Him as the King. Our way of life, ministry, and "doing church," which transgresses Kingdom law, proves this for all to see.

The problem therefore is not *charisma*, but *exousia*. If we fail our graduations, our very own desert tests, again and again, it is because we basically rebel against God's rule, act in our own best interests, and do not abide by His principles. This is such a powerful transgression that it makes us illegal aliens in God's Kingdom. In that case, no amount of begging, fasting, praying, singing, laying on of hands, or self-appointing—declaring and decreeing ourselves to be mighty miracle workers—will do the trick. Every human has been or will be tested. As David wrote, *"Search me, O God, and know my heart, try me..."* (Ps. 139:23).

Authenticity

But those who pass those tests, which are *always* tests of our loyalty to God, become legitimate. And a legitimate life, a life that does not speak or repeat hollow and cheap words, but that has been tested in the fire, ultimately becomes authentic and convicting. Words can convince, but only a life backed up by God *convicts.* Everything else will be religious hypocrisy, which the secular world rightly despises.

But when we live what we preach, it leads to *authenticity.* The whole world searches for genuineness, for the real deal. And life in God's Kingdom is very real, and therefore, very different from life in this world. It is authentic life, abundant life, life in fullness (see John 10:10).

As we can see in Jesus' life, this does not necessarily describe a materially successful, secure, rich, and healthy life that requires us to walk this earth eternally smiling like members of a triumphant cult. It means a life so overflowing with life that it reaches its goal, fulfills its mission and purpose, and is able to give life to others. Such a life cannot remain hidden and invisible because no one lives in a vacuum. It is tangible and authentic in the six main domains of life: family, education, communication, culture, business, and politics. And these are exactly the six areas in which the power of God will become evident, and difficult to ignore.

Faceless Nobodies

Jesus said, "...*Unless you are converted and become as little children, you will by no means enter the Kingdom of heaven*" (Matt. 18:3). If we are outside of the Kingdom, outside of God's stadium, we can stand with our religious songbooks, manuals, conference brochures, and visiting cards from Christian gurus who prayed over us as long as we want. Nothing will change.

But if we dare to become faceless nobodies, the loyal subjects of our King, doing as the King pleases, we will learn to swim in swarms like the fish that God created. We will learn to fly in formation as every bird in God's sky teaches us. Then truly the sky will be the limit of what such a Church under God can and will do.

This is the lesson that the non-western Christians (historically speaking, children in the faith) are today teaching the ones who originally brought the Gospel to them (their western parents, who have become the new mission field).

The Church in the cultural West today will need to stoop down and humble itself to listen and learn what its children—the Church in the non-West—are whispering back: obey your King, let go of your unholy individualism, return to being faceless (no)bodies who are attached to an incredible head—the King. Then you also will be given *exousia*, legal power to lead an explosive life in all areas, including business, politics, culture, arts, education, and family.

This is how you move from success (in human terms) to significance (in eternal terms). It happens when nobodies, who have died to self and denied their ego, become true disciples of Jesus. He makes all of us fit into that very spot that the King has designed us to fill. He enables us to fulfill our life mission, to finish well, and eventually to hear those priceless words from the mouth of the King, which make everything worth it: "*Well done, good and faithful servant...*" (Matt. 25:21).

Endnotes

1. Tony Collis, in conversation with the author; with permission.

2. *Ibid.*

3. I have written much more on this in *The Starfish Manifesto,* which is available as a free download from www.starfishportal.net.

NOTES AND APPLICATIONS

Chapter 10

REDEFINING CHURCH

Dr. Scott McDermott

THE CENTRAL MESSAGE OF JESUS was the Kingdom of God. Throughout His teaching, He called people to personal change in view of its imminence, He demonstrated its presence by His miraculous actions, and He taught about its expression for personal life and mission. To Jesus, the Kingdom of God represented the manifestation of the sovereign activity of God in which the future makes its way into the present.

One New Testament scholar says that, for Jesus, the Kingdom is "divine action…the act of God in which the kingly rule and dominion of God was clearly manifest."[1] Throughout the ministry of Jesus, we see evidence of this central message contained in the parables, beatitudes, and miracle stories, all highlighting the Kingdom of God.[2]

While the explicit naming of the Kingdom of God may recede into the background in Paul's letters, similar thinking permeates his message. The Church represents the dawning of a new age for humanity. The future is breaking into the present as manifest under the work of the Holy Spirit who Himself is the foretaste of things to come (see Eph. 1:14). From Paul's description, the Church is supernaturally empowered by God's presence for ministry now, and that empowering includes the miraculous (see 1 Cor. 12:7-11).

All of this leads us to ask if this message of Jesus and the teachings of Paul have any bearing whatsoever on our present understanding of church. I think it does, and even more so than we would realize.

Years ago, someone asked a question that I have long thought about, "What is church?" *What is church?* I thought. That's simple. It's the community of the redeemed. The fellowship of the forgiven! It's the called-out ones. But the more I considered it, the more I seriously wondered if we had not lost or forgotten a self understanding that seemed so ingrained in the earliest of Christians.

At the heart of this self understanding is the call to power ministry. I believe Jesus intended it to be foundational in practice. All too often, it has been relegated to the Church's fringe, or hidden away in a theological classroom for debate, rather than becoming part and parcel of a community meant to embody the dawning of a new age breaking into the earth.

This is clearly seen when God begins to display His power and people are healed right before our eyes. When it does occur, it may not always evoke faith and thanksgiving, but rather stir personal uncertainty or worse yet, a feeling that the miraculous is somehow foreign to God's intention for His people. Has the present day Church drifted so far from its historical moorings that it has lost its sense of supernatural ministry in this world?

I myself have witnessed the uncertainty the miraculous can evoke. In our Sunday morning services, we began to experiment with power ministry. What would happen if we stopped the service right in the middle and begin to pray for each other? Seems innocent enough, doesn't it? I mean, what could possibility happen if we asked God to heal the person sitting right next to us? Well, I'll tell you what happens. God responds! People start experiencing healing breakthroughs.

The first time we did this, we had over 20 people receive healing in our Sunday morning services. I was astounded! But I was even more astounded at some of the congregation's response. "Why are we doing this Pastor?" "Pastor, can't you just teach us and let us go home without us having to pray for each other like this?" Now I am sure, if you asked each of these people if they believed in the miraculous, they would have given a resounding "yes!" After all, healing is in the Bible! But there is a big difference between believing in *a God who did heal* and a *God who does heal.*

When God begins to truly move, it exposes areas of our lives that need repair or rebuilding. So I asked the congregation to submit a list of questions they had about healing, and from it, I taught ten weeks to help move us forward in power ministry. One of the key questions that continued to arise was, "Why do we pray for healing?"

God Commanded us to Pray for Healing

One of the main reasons we pray for healing is because Jesus told us to do so. It is part of our divine assignment. Notice the assignment Jesus gives to His disciples in Luke 9:1-2. He authorizes them to share the good news of the Kingdom of God and heal the sick.

> *When Jesus had called the Twelve together, He gave them power and authority to drive out all demons and to cure diseases, and He sent them out to preach the Kingdom of God and to heal the sick* (Luke 9:1-2 NIV).

In Luke 10, Jesus restates the same command, but this time to a larger audience of 72 of His followers by saying *"Heal the sick who are there and tell them, 'The kingdom of God is near you'"* (Luke 10:9 NIV). Notice that preaching the good news and healing the sick are linked. In essence, Jesus authorizes the disciples to "show and tell" the message of the Kingdom. The Kingdom of God as divine action releases humanity from its oppression. Power ministry as the display of God's sovereignty is an assumptive part of the proclamation of the Kingdom. Words are not to be divorced of action.[3]

The fact that Jesus commands His disciples to pray for the sick means that believers are given the authority to engage one of satan's strongholds in this present age. The word *authority* actually means "jurisdiction." It is as if Jesus is saying, "I am sending you into those places where My power has not made itself known yet. Go there and welcome My Kingdom to become manifest." The disciples clearly understood their mission of "show and tell." Luke summarizes their results in Luke 9:6. *"So they set out and went from village to village, preaching the gospel and healing people everywhere"* (NIV).

One key lesson I have learned from both Bible study and experience is that God's anointing rests upon the assignments of the Kingdom. God has already given us our agenda.[4] That means that, when I pray for healing, I am authorized to do so. Remember the Sunday morning I referred to earlier? As I took that step forward that Sunday, I reminded myself of my commissioning. This is what I have been authorized to do, so I am just going to trust Him to do it. That morning, as we launched out into the regular prayer for healing, God moved with amazing power. Many were healed. God's anointing was already resting on the assignment. All I had to do was step into it. If I want to move in God's power, then I give myself to what He assigns me to do.

Some have questioned the legitimacy of Luke 9 and 10 for contemporary ministry because power ministry is not expressly reiterated in the Great Commission (see Matt. 28:18-20). Yet this argument neglects the fundamental nature of mission and discipleship already described in the Gospels. Power ministry is not expressly reiterated in the Great Commission because it is already assumed as a part of early Christian mission.

For Matthew, discipleship and mission contain the character of miraculous activity. At one point, Matthew cites Jesus as saying: *"...Ask the Lord of the harvest, therefore, to send out workers into His harvest field"* (Matt. 9:37-38 NIV). It is clear by its context, that for Jesus those who work the harvest field are authorized to pray for healing. Miracle stories surround His request for workers, and the very next verse contains His commissioning to *"heal every disease and sickness"* (Matt. 10:1 NIV). To be a disciple is to engage in a ministry of proclamation and a display of powerful, divine action.[5]

This fact is reinforced by other books in the New Testament. In Acts for example, Peter demonstrates that the assignment of healing continues when he says to the crippled man at the gate called Beautiful, *"Silver or gold I do not have, but what I have I give you. In the name of Jesus Christ of Nazareth, walk"* (Acts 3:6 NIV). Peter acts under the authorization of the name of Jesus, which allows him to address the man's illness. But this authorization to pray for healing is not just limited to evangelistic endeavors. It is to be a part of Christian community life as well. In the book of James, believers are commanded to pray for each other's healing. What is important for us to realize is that this practice is not viewed as abnormal, but rather as a normal and customary practice. *"Therefore confess your sins to each other and pray for each other so that you may be healed. The prayer of a righteous man is powerful and effective"* (James 5:16 NIV). One can only take from this that, in the New Testament, praying for healing does not come to us as a divine suggestion, but rather as a divine expectation.

God Empowers Us to Pray

Not only does God command us to pray for healing, God also empowers us to pray for healing. This theme finds itself carefully expressed in the teachings of Jesus, the book of Acts, and the writings of Paul. Luke 9:1, for example, states that *"...He gave them **power** and authority to drive out all demons and to cure diseases"* (NIV). This verse not only underscores the ministry task at hand for the disciples, but it also foreshadows a day when they will share in the ministry of Jesus in the power of the Spirit.[6] In Acts 1:8, believers are promised "power" by the Holy Spirit for the mission, a mission that links empowered speech with power ministry.[7]

At Pentecost, the Church enters into the age of the Spirit, but it is Paul who provides us with important glimpses as to what is happening under the Spirit's enabling. In Second Corinthians 1:21-22, Paul describes the Spirit's work in this way. *"Now it is God who makes both us and you stand firm in Christ. He anointed us, set His seal of ownership on us, and put His Spirit in our hearts as a **deposit, guaranteeing what is to come"** (NIV). The Spirit brings us tomorrow *today.* As Paul says in Romans 8:23, *"Not only so, but we ourselves, who have the **firstfruits of the Spirit,** groan inwardly as we wait eagerly for our adoption as sons, the redemption of our bodies"* (NIV). Tasting of all that the Spirit brings is a small sample of what will be one day.[8]

I illustrated this concept once for my congregation during a Sunday morning service by asking them if they had ever walked down the corridor of a shopping mall, only to be captured by the aroma of chocolate chip cookies baking in the cookie shop. The sweet aroma that fills the corridors tirelessly beckons each shopper to taste and see for themselves how delicious these cookies really are.

As I gave this description during the Sunday morning message, my wife was in our church kitchen, you guessed it, baking chocolate chip cookies. Since the kitchen is located right next to our worship center, no sooner had I entered into this tantalizing description of the chocolate chip cookies and their virtues, when the aroma from the kitchen began to fill the worship center. "This is a great description" one person said, "I can even smell cookies baking!" Just then the ushers burst through the kitchen door carrying full trays of chocolate chip cookies. These warm cookies were passed down each row so everyone could taste for themselves. Everyone laughed as the cookies were passed one to the other. I then said, "Aren't they good?" They all nodded their heads in agreement. "It just leaves you wanting more doesn't it?" "Yes," they all replied.

That is how God works by His Spirit. When we taste and see what God does, He always leaves us yearning for more. That is how Paul describes the work of the Spirit in Romans 8:23. *"Not only so, but we ourselves, who have the firstfruits of the Spirit, **groan inwardly** as we wait eagerly for our adoption as sons, the redemption of our bodies"* (NIV). And then from the platform, I uncovered a giant chocolate chip cookie. "One day, you will get the whole thing, but right now, God gives us a taste of Heaven that makes us hungry for more of what He offers us." That is the way in which Paul describes the work of the Holy Spirit. He gives us a foretaste of things to come.

Gordon Fee puts it this way: "The visitation of God through the Holy Spirit establishes believers as a thoroughly eschatological people, who live the life of the future in the present as they await the consummation."[9] This means that the Church draws upon its future not only as a hope of a newer heavenly reality, but that it acts, tastes, and partakes of a dimension of that reality now. The DNA of Heaven flows through the spiritual veins of the Church God envisions. That is what makes the manifestations of the Spirit's power so amazing.

Now to each one the manifestation of the Spirit is given for the common good. To one there is given through the Spirit the message of wisdom, to another the message of knowledge by means of the same Spirit, to another faith by the same Spirit, to another gifts of healing by that one Spirit, to another miraculous powers, to another prophecy, to another distinguishing between spirits, to another speaking in different kinds of tongues, and to still another the interpretation of tongues. All these are the work of one and the same Spirit, and He gives them to each one, just as He determines (1 Corinthians 12:7-11 NIV).

These are not mere personal endowments given for personal fulfillment; instead they are endowments of anointing which draw upon tomorrow's reality today. Fee adds, "The reason for the gifts in the assembly is to build us up as we live out the life of the future in this present age."[10] Clearly in this passage, Paul highlights aspects of power ministry, especially represented by miracles and gifts of healing. Paul's description seems to indicate that these gifts of the Spirit are spontaneous, free-flowing, and given as the Spirit determines. These are spiritual endowments of supernatural enabling for the advancing of God's work in this present age, given to those who make themselves available for His working.

I have both experienced and witnessed the Spirit enabling people with supernatural power in meetings all over the world. On one hand, I am struck by the simplicity of it all, but on the other hand, I am amazed at the miracles produced out of the Spirit's enabling. One Sunday morning, I invited those needing healing prayer to indicate their need by standing or raising their hand. I asked them to remain where they were, and I invited members of the congregation who wanted to pray to join those requesting prayer.

One man, who had been attending our church for about a year and a half, was amazingly touched by God's Spirit as members of our congregation prayed for him. He had been in a wheelchair for two years, and doctors believed he would never walk again. But that

Sunday God had something else in mind. As congregants gathered around him, those praying for him were supernaturally empowered to pray. The gifts of healing began to flow. The man receiving prayer said he felt his legs strengthened, and he began to walk for the first time in two years. I can still see him walking around the perimeter of our congregation and coming down front to the platform. His wife was in tears, he was overcome with the wonder of God's grace, and the congregation was in awe of what had just taken place. God empowers us to pray!

God Cares About the Whole Person

Jesus commanded His disciples to heal the sick because God cares about the whole person. It's important to note that Jesus did not command the disciples to merely encourage and comfort the sick. To be sure, those who suffer disease need both encouragement and comfort, and this must never be neglected. But He also encourages His disciples to think of those situations with new divine possibilities.

Jesus was frequently moved with compassion for the practical needs of the people around Him, and this compassion is often associated with manifestations of healing (see Matt. 9:36; 14:14; 20:34; Mark 1:41). It is not surprising then to see Jesus respond to a family member of His inner circle. While in Capernaum, Jesus discovers that Peter's mother-in-law is stricken with a fever.

> *When Jesus came into Peter's house, He saw Peter's mother-in-law lying in bed with a fever. He touched her hand and the fever left her, and she got up and began to wait on Him* (Matthew 8:14-15 NIV).

How did Jesus respond? He healed her. He cared about her physical condition. In examining His miracles, one realizes that, for

Jesus, there was no need too big and no need too small. Whatever the need, Jesus had compassion. Matthew goes on to tell us that many came that evening to receive a healing touch from Jesus. In observing this Matthew concludes:

> *This was to fulfill what was spoken through the prophet Isaiah: "He took up our infirmities and carried our diseases"* (Matthew 8:17 NIV).

That God cares about our eternal destiny is without question! But God also cares about our life here and now. He cares about our emotional struggles and our personal hardships, and He cares about our sickness. God cares about the whole person.

This practice of praying and caring for the whole person seems to have had a profound impact for the early Church's ministry and growth, even beyond the New Testament.[11] Dr. Ramsey MacMullen makes the case that Christianity grew so rapidly in the first three centuries due to power ministry. In other words, the early Church continued to do what Jesus instructed His disciples to do. In his work, he quotes the first Church historian Eusebius who told of the role of power ministry in the growth of the early Church:

> …many…who amplified the Message, planting the saving seed of the heavenly kingdom far and wide in the world…evangelizing…with God's favor and help, since wonderful miracles were wrought by them in those times also through the Holy Spirit. As a result, assembled crowds, every man of them on the first hearing, eagerly espoused piety toward the maker of all things.[12]

Since God cares for the whole person, then I must adjust my ministry focus accordingly. When we approach those who are pre-Christian, all aspects of who they are must be in view.

I was in a restaurant when I noticed that the person working behind the counter had terrible sores on her leg. I asked her what the problem was, and she told me that she suffered from an acute case of psoriasis. It was early in the morning, and as of yet, she had no other customers except me, so I said to her: "Look, there is no one here right now; how about I pray for you?" She agreed.

When I returned to the restaurant a few days later, I inquired how she was doing. She looked over at me and said, "I have got to tell you what happened. After you prayed for me, I got much better. Now I have this other physical problem. Would you mind praying for me now about that?" "Sure," I said. Right there in the middle of a now busy restaurant, I prayed for her again. God cares about the whole person, and that means I must as well.

God Has Declared War

As we stated earlier in this chapter, the teaching of the Kingdom of God is central to the message of Jesus. All through the Gospels we find this phrase, "the Kingdom of Heaven is near." What Jesus is saying is that the Kingdom of God is about to take charge. But the teaching of Jesus actually goes beyond the mere imminence of the Kingdom. Jesus also clearly asserts that the Kingdom of God has entered the present age. In Matthew 12:28, Jesus states it this way: *"But if I drive out demons by the Spirit of God, then the kingdom of God has come upon you"* (NIV). The fact that the Kingdom of God *"has come upon you"* means that the Kingdom has now entered this present age at a particular point in time.[13]

For the early Church, this idea proved key in their own self understanding and unfolding ministry. To illustrate this, imagine two separate boxes, each representing two distinct kingdoms. On the one side stands the kingdom of satan, represented by this

187

present age. On the other side is the Kingdom of God, referred to in the Bible as the age to come. Under each of the two categories we will place the characteristics of these two kingdoms. It would look something like this:[14]

Present Time = The kingdom of satan, or satan's time	The Age to Come = The Kingdom of God
Characterized by:	Characterized by:
Sin	Righteousness
Sickness	Wholeness
Death	Resurrection
No Spirit	The Spirit

The time in which we now live is considered the present age, and it bears satan's characteristics (see Eph. 2:1-2). God's Kingdom is antithetical to everything satan's kingdom represents, as we can see in the diagram. The Bible does more than present a contrast; it tells us that God's Kingdom forcefully advances (see Matt. 11:12) against all aspects of this present age. In other words, God's Kingdom is not only antithetical to satan's kingdom, but God actually seeks to free people from the oppression of this present age.

But wait, there is more! Not only does God's Kingdom forcefully advance against this present age, but the age to come has now entered the present age, meaning that the resources reserved for the future (the age to come) are now available and breaking into the present because of the ministry of Jesus. First Corinthians 10:11 describes it this way: *"These things happened to them as examples and were written down as warnings for us, **on whom the fulfillment of the ages has come"*** (NIV). The moment is now!

While this present age will only end at the second coming of Christ, the fact that God's Kingdom has entered the present age changes our viewpoint in ministry. When it comes to praying for healing, I am able to pray in faith because I know it is God's desire to defeat everything in satan's kingdom. It was after the 72 disciples returned from a mission of healing and freeing people from demonic oppression that Jesus declared in Luke 10:18, *"I saw Satan fall like lightning from heaven"* (NIV). It is the agenda of the disciples of Jesus to dislodge satan's grip on creation.[15] The Church is satan's eviction notice, letting him know that his time is up.

A New Vision for Church

Why do we pray for healing? God opposes satan's oppression of humanity, and that means that I have been recruited by Him to advance His Kingdom on this earth. This means that power ministry is not to be on the fringe of Christian ministry or hidden away from the popular masses, lest they be offended by the acts of God. Power ministry is, in fact, representative of both God's nature and God's desire for His humanity, and as such, it should form the heart of Church life.

I was in prayer one day when I felt the Lord impress the significance of power ministry upon my life. These words seemed to flow as I began to dream about what church could become.

I dream of a church

- where people come to faith every Sunday,
- where healing flows as freely as a spring rain,
- where testimony to God's supernatural activity is a common occurrence,

- where worship attracts Heaven's attention, and prayers draw Heaven down to earth
- where teaching empowers, instructs, and revives,
- where God is at home with us, and we are at home with God, and
- where faith is contagious, love is infectious, and power is transferable.
- I dream of a church that redefines church. I dream of church the way God intended it to be. I dream that we are that church. I believe it is time to be the church God has intended the church to be. Now is the time!

Endnotes

1. John Dominc Crossan, *In Parables, The Challenge of the Historical Jesus* (New York: Harper and Row, 1973), 23.

2. John P. Meier, *A Marginal Jew: Rethinking the Historical Jesus, Vol 2: Mentor, Message, and Miracles* (New York: Doubleday, 1994), 238.

3. This is also true when it comes to the display of love and compassion (see Matt. 25:31-46).

4. I would summarize this Kingdom agenda as being four-fold: 1) calling people to a life of personal transformation (see Matt. 6:33); 2) praying for the sick (see Luke 9:1-2); 3) setting the oppressed free (see Luke 9:1-2), and 4) caring for the poor (see Matt. 11:5).

5. "His followers are to carry forward his message and his wonders..." Howard Clark Kee, *Miracle in the Early Christian World: A Study in Sociohistorical Method* (New Haven, CT: Yale University Press, 1983), 158.

6. "The same power and authority are now extended to the apostles, who will exercise them as participants in Jesus' ministry, in a way that points forward to the apostolic mission in Acts (cf. Acts 1.8)." Joel B. Greene, *The Gospel of Luke: The New international Commentary on the New Testament* (Grand Rapids, MI: Eerdmans Publishing Company, 1997), 358.

7. See Craig S. Keener, *The Spirit in the Gospels and Acts: Divine Purity and Power* (Peabody, MA: Hendrickson Publishers, 1997), 190-192 for a discussion of inspired speech and Pentecost. See also James B. Shelton, *Mighty in Word and Deed: The Role of the Holy Spirit in Luke-Acts* (Peabody, MA: Hendrickson Publishers, 1991), 78-81 for the link between speech and miracle.

8. See J. Christiann Beker, *Paul the Apostle: The Triumph of God in Life and Thought* (Philadelphia, PA: Fortress Press, 1980), 303ff.

9. Gordon Fee, *Paul, the Spirit and the People of God* (Peabody, MA: Hendrickson, 1996), 49.

10. *Ibid.,* 177.

11. This aspect of caring for the whole person also included a sense of belonging to a new family. In an age of great social migration, group identity met an important social and personal need. See Wayne A. Meeks, *First Urban Christians: The Social World of the Apostle Paul* (New Haven, CT: Yale University Press, 1983), 85-110.

12. Ramsay MacMullen, *Christianizing the Roman Empire (A.D. 100-400)* (New Haven, CT: Yale University Press, 1984), 25.

13. "He is the only Jew of ancient time known to us who preaches not only that people were on the threshold of the end of time, but that the new age of salvation had already begun." David Flusser, *Jesus* (Jerusalem: Magnes Press, 1997), 110.

14. Based on Paul Fee, 50. I would also add other categories to this table, including poverty and oppression. See Luke 4.

15. "No doubt, the successful mission of the Seventy prompts this reply of Jesus, but it is not a reply confined to their mission. Notice the mixing of tenses: "The demons are subject to us" (present); "I saw [literally, was seeing] Satan fall" (continuing past); and "Nothing shall hurt you" (future). That which has been and is taking place in Jesus' ministry and theirs will move to its completion in the future. As he so often does, Luke is undoubtedly here thinking of the mission of the church following the empowering of the Holy Spirit." F. B. Craddock, *Luke. Interpretation, A Bible commentary for Teaching and Preaching* (Louisville, KY: John Knox Press, 1990), 147.

NOTES AND APPLICATIONS

Chapter 11

LIVING FROM THE TIMELESS ZONE

Kris Vallotton

THERE IS A HUGE DIFFERENCE between living *for* eternity and living *from* eternity. Most Christians know we are supposed to live for eternity, laying up treasures in the place that transcends time and space, but very few believers seem to understand that we are also to live *from* eternity. Paul makes it clear in the book of Ephesians that we are seated in heavenly places with Christ (see Eph. 2:6). We live on this finite earth *and* in God's eternal Heaven at the same time. That's right! We simultaneously exist in two different dimensions. Now this is a difficult concept to wrap our brains around, but when our heavenly seat assignment moves from a theology to a reality, it will forever transform our destiny and create a legacy!

Understanding Eternity

Let's see if we can better understand eternity and the ramifications that the timeless zone has on our lives. Historically, we know that Jesus was crucified around two thousand years ago. But the Bible says that Jesus was slain *"from the foundation of the world"* (Rev. 13:8). How could Jesus be crucified *before* God created the world and then also have an earthly manifestation thousands of years later?

The simple answer is that God doesn't live inside time. When He said, *"Let there be light"* (see Gen. 1:3), He not only created the sun and the moon, He created *time*. You might have noticed that in the Book of Genesis, chapter one, God created night and day before He created the sun and the moon. The spirit world lives in the timeless zone.

Picture time like a train moving through eternity, the engine representing the beginning of time and the caboose signifying the end of time. Now imagine that God is able to board that finite train anywhere He wants to. He knows what's going to happen in the future because *He has already been there*. God is not bound by time because He lives in eternity. He is the one who was, the who one is, and the one who is to come, simultaneously (see Rev. 1:8). That's right; Jesus lives in the past, in the present, and in the future all at the same time. Peter put it this way, *"Do not let this one fact escape your notice, beloved, that with the Lord one day is like a thousand years, and a thousand years like one day"* (2 Pet. 3:8 NASB).

Another great example of God's eternal perspective is found in the book of Jeremiah. The Lord, speaking to Jeremiah, said, *"Before I formed you in the womb I knew you, and before you were born I consecrated you; I have appointed you a prophet to the nations"* (Jer. 1:5 NASB). But it gets even better. The great apostle Paul said, *"He chose us in Him before the foundation of the world..."* (Eph. 1:4 NASB). You may think that you were saved five years ago, ten years ago, or whenever you said yes to Jesus, but God says that He chose you before He created the world!

Praying From Heaven Toward Earth

By now you might be saying, "OK, you've convinced me that God lives in eternity and that time is a created thing. I know that this will probably matter a lot to me when I die, but what does this have to do with me now?"

I am glad you asked. The answer is *everything!* You see, if we realize that we are actually seated in Heaven with Christ, that it isn't just a metaphor or some spiritual figure of speech, then we can start to live *from* Heaven *toward* earth. For example, Jesus taught us to pray that it would be on earth as it is in Heaven (see Matt. 6:10). If we take our place with Christ, look around Heaven, and pray toward earth to replicate our celestial perspectives, we will begin to procreate with the Lord.

When we pray and intercede *from earth toward Heaven,* our posture is defensive. In other words, we are most often interceding to fix something that has already gone wrong or that we fear will transpire. Earth-bound praying subjects itself to the circum*stances* of life, and completely ignores our heavenly *stance* and the awesome authority that we have in Christ. In this weakened mindset, our earthly state of affairs commonly dictates and dominates our heavenly dialogue.

On the other hand, praying from the royal palace gives us timeless perspective, prophetic foresight, heavenly oversight, and godly insight, which causes our *words to become worlds.* This is the place where formless and void chaos suddenly becomes a beautiful planet and dead dry bones are transformed into a mighty army (see Ezek. 37:1-10). When we take our blood-bought place in Christ, we begin to pull Heaven to earth, which manifests as impossible situations being subject to the greater realities of the Kingdom. Praying from this ascended dimension allows miracles to take place. Miracles are simply the observable result of a superior Kingdom being superimposed over an inferior realm or a more highly developed ecological system breaking into this descended reality as we make prophetic declarations. Ultimately, history belongs to those who pray!

Dual Citizenship

You might be asking yourself, "If prayer is so powerful and Heaven is so available, then why does this planet seem to be in such crisis?" There are many reasons for earth's epic calamities. One of them is best articulated in the old axiom, "Earth is not my home." So many Christians mistakenly believe that Heaven is our only home and, therefore, they relegate the dominion of the earth to unbelievers. No wonder the planet is in such a mess. But what these folks have failed to realize is that the born-again experience causes us to become new creatures with *dual* citizenship. We hold legal residency and hence responsibility in both Heaven and on the earth. Let me give you a couple examples.

Jesus simply put it this way, *"Blessed are the gentle, for they shall inherit the earth"* (Matt. 5:5 NASB).

When the Pharisees tried to trick Jesus into admitting that He was only responsible to one kingdom, He wisely confronted their unfounded perspective. He let them know that they should render to Caesar—God's earthly government (see Rom. 13:1-13)—what belongs to Caesar and give to God the things that are God's! Here it is in black and white:

> *Then the Pharisees went and plotted together how they might trap Him in what He said. And they sent their disciples to Him, along with the Herodians, saying, "Teacher, we know that You are truthful and teach the way of God in truth, and defer to no one; for You are not partial to any. Tell us then, what do You*

think? Is it lawful to give a poll-tax to Caesar, or not?" But Jesus perceived their malice, and said, "Why are you testing Me, you hypocrites? Show Me the coin used for the poll-tax." And they brought Him a denarius. And He said to them, "Whose likeness and inscription is this?" They said to Him, "Caesar's." Then He said to them, "Then render to Caesar the things that are Caesar's; and to God the things that are God's" (Matthew 22:15-21 NASB).

Jesus clearly taught us to be responsible to two kingdoms.

The psalmist wrote, *"The heavens are the heavens of the Lord, but the earth He has given to the sons of men"* (Ps. 115:16 NASB).

Even the great apostle Paul, who gave us some of the most insightful revelation about our seat in heavenly places with Christ, argued that he was also an earthly citizen of Rome:

When they stretched him out with thongs, Paul said to the centurion who was standing by, "Is it lawful for you to scourge a man who is a Roman and uncondemned?" When the centurion heard this, he went to the commander and told him, saying, "What are you about to do? For this man is a Roman." The commander came and said to him, "Tell me, are you a Roman?" And he said, "Yes." The commander answered, "I acquired this citizenship with a large sum of money." And Paul said, "But I was actually born a citizen." Therefore those who were about to examine him immediately let go of him; and the commander also was afraid when he found out that he was a Roman, and because he had put him in chains (Acts 22:25-29 NASB).

Notice how Paul used his rights as a Roman citizen to help his situation, freeing himself from the centurion's beatings. Paul's earthly citizenship benefited him, which ultimately helped to advance the Kingdom of God.

History or His Story?

What I am about to tell you next may seem crazy, but it's true! I want to propose to you that, if we live from Heaven toward earth *and* we take responsibility for the planet as well as the Kingdom, history will become His story! What I am trying to say is that, when we live *from* eternity, Heaven's chronicles will actually become earth's narrative. This will result in the kingdom of this world becoming the Kingdom of our Lord and His Christ (see Rev. 11:15). After all, Jesus is Lord of all universes. The word *universe* means "one song." Jesus taught us to only sing one song (metaphorically speaking) when He said to pray, *"Your kingdom come. Your will be done on earth as it is in heaven"* (Matt. 6:10).

Destiny's Child

It is so important that we understand how our eternal reality and our earthly journey combine to create both our personal destiny and our corporate legacy. You see, our personal destiny and our corporate legacy lie in three dimensions: our history, our testimony, and our prophecy or, to put more scripturally: what was, what is, and what is to come.

We talked about how living with timeless perspectives empowers us to pray from eternity so that we are procreating *with* God and not just praying *to* God. Now let's see if we can grasp *how* exactly eternity affects life on this planet.

When we received Jesus we were granted eternal life (see John 3:16). I used to believe this meant that, from the day I asked Christ into my heart, I was assured life forever with God. Of course, it does mean that, but there is so much more. Eternal life is not only eternity that perpetuates forward into infinity, but it is also eternity that predates creation itself.

Jesus helped to clarify this when He debated with the Sadducees on the subject of the resurrection. They didn't believe that people would rise from the dead, so Jesus asked them a pointed question:

> ...Have you not read in the book of Moses, in the passage about the burning bush, how God spoke to him, saying, "I am the God of Abraham, and the God of Isaac, and the God of Jacob"? He is not the God of the dead, but of the living; you are greatly mistaken" (Mark 12:26-27 NASB).

Jesus' point of course is that Abraham, Isaac, and Jacob are *still alive.*

When we received eternal life, we came into the unity of the Spirit (see Eph. 4:3), and we became a part of the Body of Christ. But again, the spirit realm lives outside of time. The Body of Christ dwells both in the visible empire, which we perceive with our natural senses, and in the invisible world, which exists among us in another realm, dimension, or frequency. I mentioned earlier that our destiny and our legacy lie in our history, our testimony, and our prophecies. When I used the word *our,* I didn't just mean *me,* I meant the entire Body of Christ. In other words, because we already live in eternity, those who lived before us are a part of *our* history, *our* testimony, and *our* prophecies. Their lives are currently affecting and infecting *our* destiny and *our* legacy.

Abraham Tithed Into His Legacy

A great story is recounted in the book of Hebrews, which shows us how the victories of those who went before us still live on *through* us. This story takes place after Abraham rescues his nephew, Lot, in Sodom by defeating five kings. On the way home from his victory, Abraham meets Melchizedek. Melchizedek seems to have stepped through the veil of eternity and onto the battlefield because the writer of Hebrews says Melchizedek has no beginning and no end.

When Abraham meets Melchizedek, he gives a tenth of all the war spoils to this timeless priest. Here is where the story gets a little wild! Hebrews 7:10 says that, when Abraham tithed to Melchizedek, Levi also tithed to him. Abraham was the father of Isaac. Isaac was the father of Jacob, whose name was later changed to Israel. Israel had 12 sons who became 12 different tribes. Levi was one of the 12 sons of Israel. The point is, *Levi got credit in Heaven for something that his great grandfather did three generations before.* Not only that, but Abraham was a hundred years old when he had Isaac, so he never met Levi! Here is the Scripture I am referring to.

> *For this Melchizedek, king of Salem, priest of the Most High God, who met Abraham as he was returning from the slaughter of the kings and blessed him, to whom also Abraham apportioned a tenth part of **all the spoils**, was first of all, by the translation **of his name**, king of righteousness, and then also king of Salem, which is king of peace. Without father, without mother, without genealogy, having neither beginning of days nor end of life, but made like the Son of God, he remains a priest perpetually. Now observe how great this man was to whom Abraham, the patriarch, gave a tenth of the choicest spoils. And those indeed of the sons of Levi who receive the priest's office have commandment in the Law to collect a tenth from the people, that is, from their brethren, although these are descended from Abraham. But the one whose genealogy is not traced from them collected a tenth from Abraham and blessed the one who had the promises. But without any dispute the lesser is blessed by the greater. In this case mortal men receive tithes, but in that case one **receives them**, of whom it is witnessed that he lives on.*

And, so to speak, through Abraham even Levi, who received tithes, paid tithes, for he was still in the loins of his father when Melchizedek met him (Hebrews 7:1-10 NASB).

Abraham gave an offering to the Ageless One, and his generosity affected a generation that he would never see during his earthly dwelling. Consequently, Levi's destiny began in Abraham history. Maximus, in the movie *Gladiator,* understood this when he said, "What we do in life echoes in eternity!"

Creating the Future

In the third chapter of the book of Acts, there is an amazing story that demonstrates how much of our life's destiny is actually the manifestation of the prophetic declarations of those who have gone on before us.

Peter and John were going to the temple. A lame man, lying at the temple gate, begging for money, interrupted them. Peter got the man's attention and let him know that he and John were broke but that they would like to give him what they *did* posses. Before the lame man could process Peter's bold proclamation, Peter grabbed him by the arm and lifted him to his feet. The guy was instantly healed, which obviously created quite a ruckus. The people started mobbing Peter and John like they were rock stars at a huge concert. Peter quickly gathered himself and began preaching the Gospel to them, which resulted in about five thousand people being born again. But right before the multitudes were transformed into new creatures in Christ, Peter made this amazing statement,

...All the prophets who have spoken, from Samuel and his successors onward, also announced these days. It is you who are the sons of the prophets and of the covenant, which God made with

your fathers, saying to Abraham, "And in your seed all the families of the earth shall be blessed" (Acts 3:24-25 NASB).

Peter declared that the prophets of old looked into the future and spoke prophetically *"of these days."* These holy men of God prophesied that there would be an extraordinary race of people born sometime in the future. These believers would be new creatures that would actually constitute a supernatural community. They would be designed to house the Holy Spirit of God, and they would even be given the mind of Christ (see 1 Cor. 2:16). They would be sons and daughters of the King Himself, so uniquely recreated that they would essentially compose a new *holy nation* and *royal priesthood* (see 1 Pet. 2:9). They would also be granted permission to co-reign with Him forever and forever (see 2 Tim. 2:12).

Then Peter made another remarkable statement to the multitudes that had gathered there. He said, *"It is you who are the sons of the prophets."* In other words, all of the prophets, from Samuel to Christ, prophesied of these days, and we are the offspring of their prophetic proclamations! We are their sons because their prophetic declarations fathered or gave birth to us, so to speak.

The Nature of Prophecy

It is important to understand how God creates and how we have been invited to co-create with Him. When God created the world, He imagined what the world should be like. When God envisioned creation in His heart, the entire universe started to be assembled in the realm of the invisible. Then God began to speak the elements into being. For example, God would say, "Let there be light," and suddenly the invisible would become visible. The book of Hebrews puts it this way, *"By faith we understand that the worlds were prepared by the word of God, so that what is seen was not made out of things which are visible"* (Heb. 11:3 NASB).

We can see by the Genesis account of creation that God prophesied the world into existence. Prophecy has two dimensions to it: *foretelling,* which is the ability to accurately forecast the future and *forth-telling,* which is the God given ability to *cause* the future.

When Ezekiel encountered the bone yard, God required him to prophesy to the dead bones their full potential (see Ezek. 37:1-10). As the prophet spoke destiny into the valley of dry bones, they became a mighty army. There are several things that we can learn from Ezekiel's experience. First, contrary to popular opinion, prophecy is not the ability to give an accurate commentary on the dry bones. Instead, prophecy is the ability to envision the bone yard as a mighty army and then to *cause* the vision to become visible through prophetic declarations, much like God did when He created the world. When Ezekiel spoke to the bones, he was not just *foretelling*—describing the future—he was *forth-telling*—causing the future.

When the prophets of old peered into the future, they began envisioning the world through the eyes of God. However, they didn't stop there. They spoke what they saw in their spirits, and their words became our world, as we read about earlier in the book of Acts. We became the answer to our forefather's prayers and the fulfillment of their prophecies. Prophecy causes history to become His story! We are the product of those who went before us and lived from eternity, captured Heaven's perspective for our future, and called it into being.

Giving Birth to Kings

Around 900 B.C., an unnamed prophet confronted Jeroboam, who had really gone sideways with God. The prophet prophesied that a king named Josiah would be born who would destroy the alters of Baal and turn the people back to God.

Now behold, there came a man of God from Judah to Bethel by the word of the Lord, while Jeroboam was standing by the altar to burn incense. He cried against the altar by the word of the Lord, and said, "O altar, altar, thus says the Lord, 'Behold, a son shall be born to the house of David, Josiah by name; and on you he shall sacrifice the priests of the high places who burn incense on you, and human bones shall be burned on you.'" Then he gave a sign the same day, saying, "This is the sign which the Lord has spoken, 'Behold, the altar shall be split apart and the ashes which are on it shall be poured out.'" Now when the king heard the saying of the man of God, which he cried against the altar in Bethel, Jeroboam stretched out his hand from the altar, saying, "Seize him." But his hand which he stretched out against him dried up, so that he could not draw it back to himself. The altar also was split apart and the ashes were poured out from the altar, according to the sign which the man of God had given by the word of the Lord. The king said to the man of God, "Please entreat the Lord your God, and pray for me, that my hand may be restored to me." So the man of God entreated the Lord, and the king's hand was restored to him, and it became as it was before (1 Kings 13:1-6 NASB).

About 300 years later, in the year 639 B.C., a boy was born named Josiah. He became king at the age of eight. His grandfather, King Manasseh, was one of the wickedest kings who had ever lived. He killed people in cold blood, just for the sport of it, and he served idols all of his life. Josiah's father was king Amon. Amon followed in the footsteps of his father, Manasseh, doing evil and following false gods.

Josiah was eight years old when he became king, and he reigned thirty-one years in Jerusalem.... He did right in the sight of the Lord and walked in all the way of his father David, nor did he

*turn aside to the right or to the left. Now in the eighteenth year
of King Josiah, the king sent Shaphan...to the house of the
Lord saying, "Go up to Hilkiah the high priest that he may
count the money brought in to the house of the Lord.... Let
them deliver it into the hand of the workmen who have the oversight of the house of the Lord...to repair the damages of the
house.... Then Hilkiah the high priest said to Shaphan the
scribe, "I have found the book of the law in the house of the
Lord." And Hilkiah gave the book to Shaphan who read it.
Shaphan the scribe came to the king and brought back word to
the king and said, "Your servants have emptied out the money
that was found in the house, and have delivered it into the hand
of the workmen who have the oversight of the house of the
Lord." Moreover, Shaphan the scribe told the king saying,
"Hilkiah the priest has given me a book." And Shaphan read it
in the presence of the king. When the king heard the words of the
book of the law, he tore his clothes* (2 Kings 22:1-11 NASB).

At 24 years of age, Josiah began to remodel the temple that had
been decimated for three generations. In the midst of the building
project, Hilkiah the priest found a book in the temple, which likely
was the Bible. The Scriptures probably had not been read publicly
since the days of Hezekiah because the kings after him served false
gods. When Shaphan the scribe read the book to the king, Josiah
responded by tearing off his royal robes. What prompted him to
such a radical response? I believe his reaction was the result of
hearing his name read from the book written hundreds of years earlier. As Shaphan recounted the words that the unnamed prophet
spoke about him to king Jeroboam, Josiah was overwhelmed with a
sense of divine purpose and destiny.

Although he had grown up in an occult environment, his destiny was already established hundreds of years before he was born

by prophetic proclamation. In a few paragraphs of a book, Josiah discovered that his history was actually Heaven's (His) story! The chronicles of Heaven had become the narrative of earth through the life of a young king.

King Josiah's life became the product of his spiritual father, King David's legacy (see 2 Kings 22:2) and the offspring of the prophetic declaration made in 639 B.C. This is the way in which God influences the affairs of men and conducts the symphony of Heaven—in one song, the song of the Lamb.

Awakening Sleeping Intercessors

The postmodern Gospel has been altered from the original mandate to heal the sick, raise the dead, cast out demons, and preach that *"the kingdom of God has come near to you"* (Luke 10:9 NASB). Now we pray for the sick, bury the dead, don't believe in the evil influence of demons, and preach that the end of the world is near. Many have become so obsessed with the antichrist that they have lost sight of their commission in Christ to *"destroy the works of the devil"* (1 John 3:8 NASB). This has resulted in our prophecies sounding more like the *New York Times* than confident declarations of hope. It takes no faith to give an in depth commentary on the valley of dry bones! But Jesus told us to pray that it would be *"on earth as it is in heaven"* (Matt. 6:10 NASB). It seems that many Christians think Jesus taught us to pray for earth to look like Heaven, but that He didn't really want us to believe it!

In 1970, the book *The Late Great Planet Earth* was published. Three years later, I found Christ, and I was submerged into this eschatology with the rest of the Jesus Movement. Our end-time worldview looked basically like a rescue mission from a planet in tribulation. We were hoping to have the strength to resist the mark of the beast and to endure the suffering of persecution until the heavenly Helivac arrived. I never went to college because we were all convinced that the end of the world was near.

The same year that I was saved, the *Roe v. Wade* initiative was passed by the highest court in our land, making abortion legal on American soil. I believe that abortion became legal on our watch primarily because the House of Hope became the Tomb of Gloom. Before you get too mad at me, let me explain.

When the Church began to believe that the world was going to get progressively worse until Jesus returned, two primary things happened. First, we took away hope for the future by inciting verses like *"Woe to those who are pregnant and to those who are nursing babies in those days"* (Matt. 24:19 NASB) as our primary end-time mindset. After all, who wants to bring children into a world where violent, evil terrorists literally rule the world and will torture anyone who won't take their mark?

Second, this hopeless eschatology disempowered the prophets to envision the future through the eyes of God and to procreate with prophetic proclamations. This eliminated the glorious foundations for future generations to come. The Jesus People Movement became the product of *end-time charts* instead of *prophetic declarations.* This relegated intercession to hopeless "groaners" instead of to watchman who remind the Lord of His glorious promises (see Isa. 62:6-7). This is reminiscent of the disciples on the night that Jesus was betrayed. They were told to watch and pray, but instead they were sleeping from sorrow.

Now an angel from heaven appeared to Him [Jesus], strengthening Him. And being in agony He was praying very fervently; and His sweat became like drops of blood, falling down upon the ground. When He rose from prayer, He came to the disciples and found them sleeping from sorrow, and said to them, "Why are you sleeping..." (Luke 22:43-46 NASB).

Ungodly sorrow puts God's powerful Bride to sleep and disempowers her divine purpose. This relegates the world to being discipled by imposters like Judas, New Age gurus, and false religious spirits who ultimately release foreboding mindsets over our land.

But thankfully we live in a new epic season where Jesus is kissing His Bride awake so that she can capture her original mandate to co-reign with her Celestial Lover!

Notes and Applications

Chapter 12

Soaking in God's Love

Marguerite Evans

I GREW UP IN CHURCH, but the idea that God had a desire to have an intimate relationship with me and to minister to me in a sovereign way was a foreign concept. The lack of that relationship was very evident in my life. I did my Christian disciplines of reading my Bible and praying a prayer, and I tried to be good—not out of love, but duty—with little success.

I did not have a passionate, joyful heart, the freedom to be me, love for my neighbor, or any sense of destiny burning in my bones. I was very insecure; I did not know who I was or where I was going. My heart was Fatherless. Children know who they are when they know their Father. I had no idea who my heavenly Father was.

The idea that I had a Father in Heaven who is absolutely crazy about me and treasures spending time with me, never even crossed my mind. It wasn't until I started to meet with Him face-to-face, heart-to-heart, that He was able to start changing the very core of who I am. As Paul wrote, *"The Spirit Himself bears witness with our spirit that we are children of God"* (Rom. 8:16).

Soaking Prayer

"Soaking Prayer, what is that?" one woman asked. "Do I need to bring my swimsuit?"

213

Like many, she had no grid for the sort of prayer that has become such a significant part of my life. The term *soaking prayer* has caused many different reactions. For those who understand the concept, it has become life changing.

Soaking prayer is our effort to explain to a do-do-do culture what it is to just be-be-be. The whole point is simply *being* with the One who created you for relationship; only from that intimate relationship will a fruitful life flow. Our relationship with Him, like any other, must be cultivated daily—and it must be two-way. That's what soaking is all about—learning to not just talk at God but to wait before Him and listen to His voice, resting in His Presence.

The concept of soaking prayer is nothing new. During previous revivals, people referred to it as "waiting on the Lord" or "tarrying" as they lingered, expecting God to touch them. Soaking includes waiting, but there is so much more. We choose to *rest* in His love rather than to strive in prayer. It is an *active* rest; we wait expectantly.

Soaking prayer time is spending time with God, like being marinated in His love. You can actually feel God loving you. Marinating a steak changes its flavor. Esther in the Bible prepared herself to meet the king with beauty treatments that included one year of soaking in different kinds of spices. In the same way, as I just rest and reflect in my heavenly Father's unconditional love, my heart softens.

As the psalmist says, *"Rest in the Lord, and wait patiently for Him..."* (Ps. 37:7).

When we pray, we often wonder whether we're even worthy to enter His presence, whether the Creator of the universe has time to just sit with us and pour into us. Does He care about the issues of my heart, the questions that I have, the dreams that I have, the potential that I have, the healing that I need? Who is He? What does He think about me? Does He have a plan for my life? God's answers to those questions are life-changing, life-transforming, and revolutionizing. When we soak, we take time to listen for His answers.

Soaking prayer is also about learning to come to Him for Him, for His heart, learning to adore Him, learning to get lost in Him. We lay down our own ideas and agendas in order to focus on Him. In that place of resting, of being vulnerable and open to Him, of getting to know Him and being known by Him, our hearts capture the answers to our life questions. I am amazed by the simplicity of connecting heart-to-heart with my Maker. We want to be so sophisticated, but it is very simple.

When our hearts—the hidden, hard, dry, disappointed, lost, underperforming, hurt, and squelched parts—start to receive the first splash of the river of His love, the revelation moves from our minds to our hearts. And God captures and heals the human heart with the power of His love!

Come to Me, all you who labor and are heavy laden, and I will give you rest. Take My yoke upon you and learn from Me, for I am gentle and lowly in heart, and you will find rest for your souls. For My yoke is easy and My burden is light (Matthew 11:28-30).

Psalm 46:10 says, *"Be still, and know that I am God...."* There is so much noise around us, and inside we constantly think of things to do. We need to give ourselves permission to take time for ourselves, time when we can be still, focus on the Lord, and listen to His voice. Then is when our hearts will receive the revelation of who God is and who we are in Him.

The result is that you will know God more intimately. It's not being still and knowing *about* God, but getting to know His heart.

We must take time alone with Him, time to just *be* in His presence in order to have more of His presence in our daily lives.

Testimonies From Soaking Prayer

Soaking prayer, as I have defined and discussed it in this chapter, began at Toronto Airport Christian Fellowship (TACF) during the revival—"The Toronto Blessing"—that God continues to pour out there.

John and Carol Arnott, founding pastors of TACF and Catch the Fire Ministries, noticed that when people went down in the power of the Spirit, God's presence would increase as they continued to stay in God's presence. Most miracles happened after people received prayer and were soaking in God's presence. After awhile they realized that they could deliberately lie down in God's presence and God would faithfully come.

Eventually soaking rooms were organized as places where people can spend as long as they need before the Lord. Today there are soaking prayer centers in churches of different denominations, homes, schools, prisons, during lunch hours, and the list goes on. We've received very powerful testimonies from a prison where angry, hurting men's lives are changing—they are being transformed from the inside out. Following are testimonies from just a few of the many people who have been forever impacted by soaking prayer.

Bill Boone

I went to the *Father Loves You Conference* and *Soaking Prayer School* at Toronto Airport Christian Fellowship (TACF). Though the revival at TACF was not new to me, what I encountered there forever changed my life.

Months prior to arriving at the conference, I found myself hungering and wanting more of Him and declaring daily what I wanted Him to do in my life when I was there.

Once there, I hungered to spend time with Him during the soaking sessions and couldn't wait until the teaching was done to soak. From the very first session, during those times of soaking, my body vibrated and shook as the presence of God overcame and filled me. After soaking for three days, three times a day, one hour per session, I went to walk out to go to dinner, and the presence of God came with an incredible force and knocked me down to the floor laughing as I've done years before, but this time it was like an enormous hand had come out of Heaven and was tickling me. I was overwhelmed with a sense of love and playfulness coming from a side of God that I had never experienced before. It was like a Daddy coming to play with me. That was very foreign to me, as I have no memories of my fathers (biological and stepfather) ever playing with me.

Two days later, during a workshop with Carol Arnott [one of the leaders at TACF], the presence of God came into the room and people began to weep and wail, and to my surprise, I was one of them. During that experience, it was like incredible waves of love totally overwhelmed me. It felt like my newfound heavenly Daddy was hugging and kissing me (which I also don't remember ever having experienced).

After 46 years of life, and 24 years of that as a Christian, I finally found the One I had always been looking for: my

Heavenly Daddy...always very close to me, but never truly experienced until that week at TACF.

Cathy Smith

During a very difficult time in my life, I was introduced to Soaking Prayer. I had never heard of it, but I was willing to do anything. After attending a Soaking Prayer meeting for about a month, I realized my heart was getting much softer. I attended a Soaking Prayer School, and I began to realize how much my Father in Heaven loved me. The Lord spent much time telling me how much He loved me and how special I was to Him. I had not had that kind of revelation in all my years of being a Christian. During the school, the Lord [showed] me something that would change me forever.

The second day of the school, there was a teaching on forgiveness and judgment. The Lord showed me that the reason that I had been in a very difficult season was that I had become very critical against the leadership in my church. There were times that I would sit with other people and tear down the leadership of the church. I would discuss all the short comings and how the direction they were going in was wrong. This went on for months. Somehow I thought I was right and they were wrong. What the Lord showed me changed my heart.

Remember, first He showed me how much He loved me. I became very secure in His love for me. The next day He showed me that my judgment toward the leadership was sin and [that] it grieved Him because He died for them and I was tearing them down. He told me that this was why my heart had become so hard. I began to weep and repent for all that I had done. I realized that I was forgiven, but I needed to make it right with the pastors of my church.

Immediately I called the pastor of the church and had conversation with him on the phone. After many tears, he was so gracious with me, forgave me, and then prayed over me. Since then, I was able to talk with him and his wife face-to-face and repent to them together. They were both very kind and quick to forgive.

Several years before, my husband was asked to be an elder in the church and we served as an elder couple. We continued to serve on the leadership team for the next four years before the Lord led us in another direction. We received a blessing from the other leaders.

Wendy Lassiter

I had struggled with depression for many years and had pretty much resolved myself to just existing day by day the best I could. While sitting in my living room one afternoon, the Holy Spirit spoke to me that I fellowshipped with the television more than I did with him. So I turned off the television and decided to spend time alone with God and see what He meant by what He said. As I began to wait on the Lord, He came with His Presence into our home and began to do a mighty healing in me. He dealt with a lot of my sinful heart issues and brooded over me and healed me while I just waited on him. Then he began to do the same thing in my husband and now our children are experiencing His love. I actually waited on the Lord in my home for about eight months before I heard the word *soaking* and realized that I had been soaking in His presence this whole time. I had experienced a great measure of healing from depression. About eight months after experiencing the Lord's love and presence like this, I attended a TACF conference for the first time ever. *The Father Loves You* was the title. During the last night, I went through a prayer tunnel, and after exiting the tunnel, I was hit by an invisible arrow from the right upper area above me. I began to laugh hysterically and did so for the next two or three hours. I tried to wake up the next morning and go to church, but couldn't stop laughing and was sort of immobilized, so I stayed in the bed laughing for the next six hours. It took about nine days for me to regain my composure so I could function properly. I know now the fruit from that encounter with God's joy has been healing in the emotions. From that time on, we have been spending lots and lots of time soaking in God's presence. We started a soaking center in our church two and a half years ago and have ministered to nearly a thousand people over that time period—some go to other local churches, some come to visit relatives from out of town, etc. Our marriage was restored; I subsequently "released" my psychiatrist and asked my family doctor to oversee my health because I was no longer experiencing any of the symptoms that had deemed me disabled in my past. My family doctor agreed that he would oversee me, and if I experienced any problems, I could go back to the psychiatrist. That was two years ago. I also wrote social services and relinquished my disability income because I was no longer willing to wear that label. I still have that letter too. For the last two years, I have earned about 16 times what I used to get when I received disability checks. Since that time, we have done nothing but continue to move closer and closer in to Father God's heart, and we desire to grow in our understanding of who He is.

Lucas Shiflet

I was born and raised in Baytown, Texas, near Houston. I was raised going to church, but it seemed to me there were a lot of rules and stuff and not much love, so I didn't really get too much out of it.

In my teens, I fell into rebellion and got way into drugs, sex, and rock 'n roll. I was lead singer of a heavy metal band which was gaining popularity. We had a bit of a following, and were even getting some record companies interested. I was partying pretty heavily. If I ever brought a girl home, my dad would say, "I don't need to remember your name, because I'll never see you again."

All this time, my mom was praying for me. She was always going to renewal/river meetings, and at the time was visiting a church (Sweetwater Christian Fellowship) that talked about the love of the Father, and was associated with TACF. She was invited to go on their group trip to Toronto to a *Soaking in God's Glory* conference. She decided to take me along.

I loved the worship at the conference, and I jumped right into it. I felt the presence of the Lord there in such a strong way. The Lord really touched my heart. I decided right then that I wanted to go to the school of ministry, even though I was still living for the devil.

However, when I got back home to Houston, I was still in the band and partying. One night, I was at a hotel party (a bunch of us would rent a hotel room and stay all night using drugs and alcohol). That night, I took so many different drugs that I overdosed. I really thought I was going to die. I cried out to God, and He answered me with His love.

Slowly, after that night, the Lord began really calling my heart. I made a decision to give up the band. They were all pretty mad at me, but I knew I had to do it. I stopped doing drugs and all the partying. I decided to live for the Lord.

Since then, I went to the school of ministry in Toronto, and the Lord did an overhaul in my heart. I learned about His amazing love for us as Daddy. And I learned that I can get in His presence any time and just soak Him in. I am now interning and lead worship at the same church that my mom was visiting back then. My whole family goes to that church. We have "soaking nights" on Friday nights, and I play keyboard and sing for the Lord. I love soaking, and I love leading other people into the presence of our Daddy also. On these nights, the presence of the Lord is amazing. And there is no place else I would rather be than in His presence.

Paula Pendleton

We live in Fairhope, Alabama. When I first started soaking in my Heavenly Father's love, I noticed that my childhood fears were disappearing. My heart cry was for "more love, Lord." The more of God's love I received, the more

I could give away to others. We have been soaking in God's presence daily for over five years and have hosted a soaking prayer group once a week on Thursdays in our home that long also.

As we arrived home from a mission trip to Pemba, Mozambique, I was rushed to the hospital emergency room and was admitted immediately. While they were doing their tests, I was soaking in God's arms. There was never a fear or concern. Diagnosed with stage 4 lymphoma cancer in April last year, I was given chemo treatments but was not expected to survive more than six months. My husband would lay his hands on me and soak me in God's loving presence, and I felt the Father hold me in His loving arms, and His love sustained me during the entire ordeal.

My last checkup was very exciting as the doctors came in shaking their heads. "Whatever you are doing," they said, "keep it up!" I give my healing Jesus all the glory, and I love my heavenly Father with all my heart, with all my soul, and with all my strength for healing me body, soul, and spirit.

Dale Moyer

My husband, Mark, and I started a Soaking Prayer Center in our home a year ago in March. It has been a wonderful journey. We have a small band from four to 12 come every Tuesday night and rest in the Lord. The more of the Lord we get, the more we want; this is a life-giving addiction.

My right shoulder was healed after two years of pain that limited me from playing my guitar or reaching behind my back. I went to a chiropractor but without any relief. Gary came over and laid his hand on my shoulder, and it felt like a cool refreshing river flowing all through me starting at my shoulder. He said God kept telling him to go and pray for me. He said he didn't even know what to pray, so he said nothing. I am so thankful he was obedient. The pain was gone. I immediately got my guitar, which I hadn't played in a long while, and started worshiping. I was so excited.

Jack Difato

I have learned that you can have a great soaking time in as little as 15 minutes—anywhere. I even soak during my PET scans! I'm currently on daily oral chemotherapy, and every six months I am scanned to check for any recurrence of cancer. Just a few weeks ago, I was having a PET scan, which requires an injection of a radioactive glucose solution. For 90 minutes I sit in a dark room waiting for the solution to disperse throughout my body. That's when the soaking begins. Next I lie on the scanning bed and am progressively moved through something that resembles a double donut. It takes about 30 minutes and you can't move while you're in there. Sometimes people think there is something wrong with me. But I like to think that there is something so right going on.

When I lie down in that scanner, I'm so at peace that they have to speak to me over the intercom and tell me it's over. I just fall back into my Heavenly Daddy's arms and soak in His Presence the entire time. I give everything over to Him because He is completely trustworthy. I do not fear the scan or the outcome because the experience of His love drives out all fear. The time goes by so quickly because I'm engulfed in my Daddy's presence. It's not that He has told me that I will never have cancer again or not be sick, but that no matter what happens He will be there with me. This is not just something I know in my head, because as I soak, head knowledge is transformed into an experience I actually live. The scan results were NED (no evidence of disease). I have now been cancer free for 5 years!

David Costello

I've been a professional artist all my life, so I'm very much aware of the struggle that takes place for "inspiration." It is the artist's ultimate desire to produce some thing meaningful that will touch the lives of others and point to something larger than oneself.

How an artist can accomplish this "without God" by his or her side must be extremely difficult if not impossible—I know because I tried for many years before giving my life to the Lord. Today I need not search for "inspiration"; it finds me—it surrounds me.

Soaking is an integral component of my "creative process" today. Everything I do flows out of resting in His presence. I don't soak with the purpose of "getting" anything from the Lord; I just soak to be in His presence, but often He will give me visions during that time. The best example of this happened some years ago when I was soaking at our home soaking group.

While simply resting in his presence, suddenly, in a matter of seconds, I received seven visions downloaded to my spirit. Instantly I knew that the seven images were meant to become a series of artwork—The "Days of Creation." This project kept me busy for the next 18 months, but the birthing of it took only a few seconds in His presence—soaking.

Behruz Darogaa

I was laid off in April 2005. I experienced shock, dismay, and despair. The Lord told me to soak for one hour a day. This I did. At a family conference, the children asked if they could have a hot dog for lunch. I had packed some hot cross buns and cheese for lunch. I was about to say this is not the time to spend money on hot dogs. But the Lord stopped me and said to "eat cheese."

Anyone familiar with Heidi Baker's testimony would know the Lord was saying not to be careful, but not to be extravagant either. So I asked the children if they would like to eat at Swiss Chalet. Their jaws dropped and their eyes were wide open.

Shortly after, one morning, as I was soaking, the Lord told me to look at gold. So I looked at the chart for gold stocks, and it was my turn for my jaw to drop and my eyes to open wide. The chart showed the biggest, most bullish textbook pattern I have seen. I put all of the severance package (about a year's salary) into gold. A year later, when I was still soaking, the Lord said, you have not looked at the chart recently. I almost gasped when I looked. The stock was very extended, and I sold for a return of 80 percent. Two weeks later, they crashed and did not reach the same levels until 18 months later.

By the end of 2006, I was able to go to Randy Clark's school of healing, the family conference, buy new bicycles for my two sons, buy a new mattress, buy eye glasses for the whole family, and even [buy] a 2000 Honda Odyssey to replace the car that was written off in a crash. After all this, my savings were the same as before I was laid off. And I still had the severance package on top of that. The leadership has said that the 90 percent that's left after tithing will go further than the 100 percent. In my experience, that's not true. In my experience zero percent can go further than 100 percent.

The Lord is also giving me ideas for inventions. All this the Lord showed me while I was soaking.

Mary Tucker

Since my initial visit to the Soaking Prayer Center in my area, over two months ago, I've noticed an insatiable hunger for God that has drawn me deeper into His heart. His breath is at times felt upon my spirit. This place has caused me to grow in a different dimension. I appreciate this place and the prayer team who covers us each Monday.

* * * *

A Transformed Life

Truly, when the revelation of God's love moves from our heads to our hearts, a person is changed, a city can be changed, a nation can be changed, and the world can be changed! A heart that is passionate about Jesus, wrecked by His love, can never turn back! Once your heart has tasted unconditional love, a love that says: "I am enough, I don't have to be someone else or perform to be loved" and "I am completely accepted," hunger is birthed within you; you want more, and more is always available! The fruit of true encounter is a heart that will go out to a dying world. Lovers are better workers than servants!

There is incredible power in His presence—the power to restore, revive, renew, revolutionize. It is possible; Jesus paid for it all. How beautiful is a transformed life! As the psalmist wrote, *"Then our mouth was filled with laughter, and our tongue with singing..."* (Ps. 126:2).

Cultivate Intimacy

Soaking prayer is not a replacement for reading the Bible, praying, intercession, Christian counseling, or any other Christian discipline. It is the other side of the conversation, cultivating intimacy, going after God's heart. Then He comes with His hand!

I have especially seen this in healing ministry. Healing of issues of the heart, like physical healing, sometimes comes in an instant. But sometimes the healing takes place over a period of time. This is where soaking comes in.

Many healing rooms and counselors have a place for their clients to soak before and after sessions with much fruit.

We've seen over and over that most of what God does happens when people stay on the floor (or sit in a chair) and keep on receiving, lingering in His presence. We so easily want "McJesus," but He wants to dine with us! There is always more! Don't miss it! When you are in that place, He has your full attention, and you have His.

Many churches have added soaking prayer to all aspects of church life. Imagine if your worship team took time to soak in God's presence before Sunday morning worship, if the intercessors, the children's ministry, the youth ministry, the hospital visit team, and so forth, all soaked before ministering. They would start from a different place. And they'd see much more fruit because they'd be working from a place of His agenda, His heartbeat, and His ever-increasing presence. He loves hearts that come to receive from Him first so that they can pour out His heart and character, not just their human efforts.

The Lord one time told me that soaking prayer centers create a place for the habitation (not just a visitation) of His presence. You can have this in your house, your office, church, the old age home in your area, shelters, etc. There are even soaking prayer centers in prisons and prisoners' lives are being transformed! Room 113 in a prison in Pennsylvania is a very special place for the inmates. Many of their lives have been transformed by the Father's love. Soaking prayer softens hearts and can even crumble walls made out of steel—that is the power of God's love.

There are no pain, addictions, lack, poverty, or sicknesses in Heaven!

Creativity in His Presence

He is *the* Creator. As children of God, we have *access*—access to the creativity of the God who created the universe. It's no wonder that, when we take time to just be with Him, He shares secrets with us in the secret place. His heart is to share with us ideas, inventions, poetry, pictures to paint, songs to sing. His heart is longing for a people who will take the time to give ourselves to Him to listen, feel, see, taste, and smell.

> *And do not present your members as instruments of unright-*
> *eousness to sin, but present yourselves to God as being alive*
> *from the dead, and your members as instruments of righteous-*
> *ness to God* (Romans 6:13).

This time with Him is so powerful and worth fighting for when life demands our time. When we take time to rest first, the power will be there to do what we need to do, with much fruit and more ease.

> *There remains therefore a rest for the people of God. For he who*
> *has entered His rest has himself also ceased from his works as*
> *God did from His. Let us therefore be diligent to enter that*
> *rest...* (Hebrews 4:9-11).

When we see from His perspective, life looks very different. Mark 1:15 says, *"The time is fulfilled, and the Kingdom of God is at hand. Repent, and believe in the Gospel."* Jesus did say that we need to "repent," which means change our way of thinking. He came, and He brought His Kingdom with Him! What a Kingdom it is! You have access!

God wants to prosper His kids, and He is giving new ideas and inventions to those who take time to fellowship and listen. As we receive in His presence, we must remember to also seek council from His Word (the Bible), prophetic words, the leaders He has placed in our lives, friends, family, etc. It is important, when the Lord gives us a directional word, to submit it to people we know who hear His voice in order to receive confirmation. *"...The sheep follow Him, for they know His voice"* (John 10:4). *"...Watch to see what He will say to me..."* (Hab. 2:1).

How to Soak

As I explained, when we soak we focus on Jesus and rest in His presence. We can also "soak" one another! I have many times been privileged to soak people. To soak someone, you put your hand gently on a safe place, like the shoulder, and focus on His presence. Remember, we enter into His presence by faith. You bless what He is doing in that person's life. This is not a time to pray necessarily but a time to step into His presence. God's power increases when we serve one another in this way.

We need more than just a prayer; we need His presence! One of the most beautiful things is seeing the Lord touching a person's life, seeing Him use us to touch one another. Many times I've seen someone receive prayer and have a minimal amount of healing or breakthrough. But after a time of soaking in His presence, that person receives complete breakthrough or healing. We've soaked people for hours. It's that important. How beautiful is the face of a transformed heart, shining with the glory of God!

Take time everyday to just be with Him. You may want to start with just ten minutes, but you can go longer. Put gentle worship music on, if you want, focus on Him, and just rest. Write down on a piece of paper all of the things that come to your mind that you need to remember to do. That will help you to rest and focus on the Lord. Sometimes He'll show you a picture or a vision, or He'll say something to you or just lavish His love on you. Other times He may show you a painful memory and help you release all of the pain, show you the people you need to forgive, and repent for your ungodly responses, or any other hindrances that may keep His love from flowing in your life. Other times He may heal your body, give you strength, convict you of sin, or release creative ideas—what He desires to give you at that moment. He knows best what you need.

You may feel the tangible presence of God or sometimes His peace. It is not about feeling, but we were created to feel and experience love. Imagine not feeling the love you have for your spouse, your children, your friends. We can feel God's love! It is not about what happens; it is about us taking the time because He is worth it, and He knows what we need. Sometimes it may feel like nothing "happened" at all, but when you give your time like that, He will touch your heart.

You can trust that the Holy Spirit is working. Remember, everything that we receive from God we receive by faith. Faith must be positive and focused on God. (Not negative and fearful, focused on the enemy). Jesus said in Luke 11:11-13:

> If a son asks for bread from any father among you, will he give him a stone? Or if he asks for a fish, will he give him a serpent instead of a fish? Or if he asks for an egg, will he offer him a scorpion? If you then, being evil, know how to give good gifts to your children, how much more will your heavenly Father give the Holy Spirit to those who ask Him!

The key is intimacy. It is not a program to be run and managed, but a relationship to be maintained.

> But without faith it is impossible to please Him, because anyone who comes to God must believe that He is, and that He is a rewarder of those who diligently seek Him (Hebrews 11:6).

Great Commandment First

My prayer is for the Lord to continue to increase the hunger for more of Him so that we'll never be complacent about where we are. We live in a time when we need to know what He thinks, what His heart beat is. We cannot let our agendas get in the way of His power moving in and through us.

The world is desperate to see real power, real answers, and as we learn to receive from Him daily, that power will flow through us to others and into our circumstances. I believe the time has come when, like Peter, our shadows will heal people (see Acts 5:15).

When we spend time with Him first, we are in step with Him, we feel His heartbeat, and we see people through His eyes.

Love is what sets us apart. As we marinate in His presence, we will receive His love. Our capacity to love our enemies, those who have hurt us, and those who require extra grace from us will increase. God will take away the stumbling blocks so that we are able to love without seeing the issues and package. Instead, His presence will give us the power to love others by seeing their potential and their heart's cry for love, which has so often shut down because of the cares of life.

We must pursue the Great Commandment first.

Jesus replied: "'Love the Lord your God with all your heart and with all your soul and with all your mind.' This is the first and greatest commandment. And the second is like it: 'Love your neighbor as yourself'" (Matthew 22:37-39 NIV).

The Great Commission comes second: *"Go into all the world and preach the good news to all creation"* (Mark 16:15 NIV).

The Beginning, Not an End

Soaking prayer is the beginning, not an end in itself. From lying down in His presence, we stand up to move into what He has for us to do with His empowering. We need to act as He leads. Soaking prayer leads to fruitfulness. You receive and then give it away to impact your spheres of influence.

Soaking leads to action.

Being with Him is the most important thing that we can do for our daily and future destiny. God's heart is to conform us to the image of His Son. Life will have its trials and testings—and I don't say that lightly—but God is good, and as our hearts receive the revelation of the heart of God, of His love, our perspective on life changes.

The revelation of the Father's heart gave me wings to fly because I discovered that I can never fall beyond His arms.

Because of the power of that revelation, I've been able to take big risks. One day I was lying on my bed in South Africa. The Lord told me to "go to Toronto now." In the natural, it was the craziest thing; it was impossible in many different ways. But I knew my Father's voice, and because I knew I could never fall beyond His arms, I boldly took that first step. My heavenly Father has had me take many more steps, and because of that I am here today writing this chapter. The journey continues...

For from days of old they have not heard or perceived by ear, nor has the eye seen a God besides You. Who acts in behalf of the one who waits for Him (Isaiah 64:4 NASB).

Thank you Jesus, all the glory and honor belong to You, my King!

NOTES AND APPLICATIONS

Conclusion

HOW TO EXTERMINATE CHURCH MICE

(*Creating a Church Where Ministry Is Learned, Practiced, and Exported*)

T HE AUTHORS OF THIS BOOK have given us all food for thought regarding how we can and should allow God's presence and power to flow through us to impact a hurting and dying world. Why is this message so vital today? Simple observation reveals that, despite what the Scriptures exhort, and what this book's authors compel us to do, the members of many churches, for various reasons, do not minister to each other when they meet together.

Consequently, the church or fellowship is usually quiet, except when the pastor delivers a sermon to the hungry flock. After the sermon, the pastor usually suggests that, if anyone needs or wants prayer, he or she can come up to the front, and someone on the prayer team will pray for them (that's if the church has a prayer team—in some cases, it may be the elders).

The Corinthian Example

In Corinth, church life involved people ministering to each other with the spiritual gifts so much that Paul had to encourage

237

them to minister *"decently and in order"* (1 Cor. 14:40). It is interesting, for several reasons, that he didn't tell them to stop their ministry activities.

First, the church in Corinth was not a place of much spiritual maturity, as the opening chapters of First Corinthians reveal. Paul called them babes in Christ, incapable of handling the meatier matters of the Christian life (see 1 Cor. 3:1-2). They caused divisions among themselves by carnally following various leaders, such as Paul, Cephas (Peter), and Apollos (see 1 Cor. 3:3-7). And they put up with sexual immorality in their midst (see 1 Cor. 5:1-8).

Second, in most fellowships today, only leaders and the spiritually mature "get to play" (a phrase coined by John Wimber). This is in stark contrast with what Paul allowed to occur in Corinth. In First Corinthians 12-14, Paul adamantly encouraged all of the folks in gatherings to minister. He even went so far as to address the issues of those who felt spiritually superior (see 1 Cor. 12:21-23) and those who felt spiritually incapable (see 1 Cor. 12:14-18).

So, contrary to modern ecclesiastical procedures, the Corinthian model of church "services" envisions a place where every believer, mature or not, is allowed in some way to minister with God's given gifts, even if that person still has deep issues that still need to be resolved.

But is this what is experienced in churches today? Do churches allow congregants the freedom to minister to one another at some point during a gathering? I hesitate to say it, but I believe the answer is no. Perhaps if someone has a Ph.D. he or she can teach or preach. Maybe if someone has proven themselves to be prophetically gifted in the past, the leadership will allow them to encourage the people with words or ideas given by the Holy Spirit. In some cases, if a person has done tasks such as clean the bathrooms or vacuum the carpeting, he or she will be allowed to usher.

Body Ministry

I believe something is wrong with this model of church life. On any given Sunday, it is likely that more than just a few folks have something to share with the church to edify and encourage it.

Paul seemed to believe this when he said,

> *How is it then, brethren? Whenever you come together, each of you has a psalm, has a teaching, has a tongue, has a revelation, has an interpretation. Let all things be done for edification* (1 Corinthians 14:26).

I'm not a church planter or an administrator, but I think today's churches need to find ways to give believers opportunities to minister *"decently and in order"* in their gatherings. This may be foreign and seem unmanageable to many leaders, so only the Holy Spirit can direct each individual church in the steps that can be taken to allow "body ministry" to occur. And only the leadership can implement those steps.

Church members who cause a commotion by going against the church's current fellowship model and try to minister outside of established parameters may believe that what they are doing is what Paul encouraged. The truth is, however, that they are being disruptive to the *current* flow of the Spirit's leading in that church. Until the Holy Spirit initiates change with the leadership's cooperation, believers should follow the current practices of their church.

Church Mice

What about those churches whose leadership does not stifle body ministry? I've been in several, and even in those places where believers are allowed to minister, a lot of believers do not. It seems that most members and attendees of church gatherings are as quiet as church mice—a malady I call *"church-icus mice-icus."* The cause of this malady may be as varied as the churches themselves. However, churches and fellowships should be places where body ministry occurs.

Church-goers who find those activities disruptive can voice their concerns to the leadership. At the same time, they should study First Corinthians 12-14 to see how Paul encouraged the Corinthian church to function *"decently and in order"* so that everyone would be edified and encouraged.

SCREAM

The church's leadership can address and cure this problem of having church mice in a congregation by employing a method I call SCREAM. Each of the points in this acronym can be greatly expanded upon biblically. I would encourage leaders to do so when they can, but for now, I will briefly comment on them.

S: Stir up

Stir up the church members and attendees to want to be used by God in ministry. Like a fire, sometimes the gift or calling in a believer's life needs to be stoked. Paul admonished Timothy, *"Therefore I remind you to stir up the gift of God which is in you through the laying on of my hands"* (2 Tim. 1:6).

Paul told Timothy to stir up the gift himself, but he didn't elaborate on how Timothy was to do that. A clue may be found later when Paul told him, *"But you be watchful in all things, endure afflictions, do the work of an evangelist, fulfill your ministry"* (2 Tim. 4:5).

It's possible that the very use of a gift, no matter how insignificant that usage may appear, can actually light a fire in your spirit, causing you to use your gifting or calling more often. Whatever the case, just as Paul encouraged Timothy to "stir up" God's gifting in him, today's leaders can stir up their congregants as well, maybe by simply reminding them to fulfill whatever ministry God has given them. This touches upon the next step.

C: Connect

Connect with the members to help them discover the giftings in which each should function with God's leading. Leaders can help facilitate the ministry of each believer by providing methods, classes, or other ways to help each person find his or her particular calling and gifting. Once someone is stirred up to be used in ministry, it is of the utmost importance to help that individual find out exactly what God has gifted them to do for the benefit of the church.

Some churches encourage folks to become part of a small group where they can experiment in ministry to see what "works" for them. Some churches have spiritual gift tests or classes to help people discover their gifts. The challenge is for church leadership to implement some method within their church's ministry model to help congregants find their gifts and callings.

R: Ratify

Ratify (approve) a culture of acceptance in the church fellowship for body ministry. A church needs to provide an atmosphere of approval of believers being used in their gifts, whether during the church service, after the church service, or in small groups. This atmosphere must radiate the belief that believers ministering to believers is normative. Somehow, the leadership should make it perfectly clear that the church is a place where, as John Wimber said, "everyone gets to play."

When it comes to ministry, no one is above another in practical importance, and no one is unneeded. Every part of the Body needs to function in its role for a church to grow:

from whom the whole body, joined and knit together by what every joint supplies, according to the effective working by which every part does its share, causes growth of the body for the edifying of itself in love (Ephesians 4:16).

When this is taking place, the church members will mature and consequently function as God's "Kingdom bringers," not only to their own hurting brethren, but also to the lost and dying world in which they live.

E: Equip/Educate

Equip and educate the members of the church to function in their individual roles, gifts, and callings. This is an offshoot of step two (Connect), since in this step, the person is mentored in the usage of their discovered gifting or calling.

This might entail the leadership pairing them up with someone who has the same gifting or calling, but who has been operating in it for a longer time. It could involve one-on-one instruction or some sort of hands-on training. However the church decides to equip and educate folks in their roles, it needs to be done persistently, and it needs to include new believers also.

A: Activate

Activate the church members and their ministries by giving them opportunities to function in the context of a church fellowship, where taking risks is not too risky. Activation naturally follows education. Believers need to have opportunities to explore their gift's unique qualities by using them. And the best and safest place to do this is in a church whose culture allows for "practice."

Gifts are most likely not given in a totally mature state. As believers grow in Christ, their giftings also grow and mature over time, and this growth is greatly accelerated when those gifts are being continuously used. So church leaders need to provide outlets for believers to exercise their individual gifts in the safety net of a loving community.

Can the leadership make time during the church service for folks to experiment? That is up to the leaders, but I would advise them to make that decision while in counsel with the Holy Spirit and God's Word. A church that has never allowed open ministry would be taking a very provocative step, so it should only be attempted through the guidance of God's Spirit and diligent adherence to Scriptural guidelines.

M: Motivate

Motivate the members of the church to move out of their comfort zones to minister wherever they go. Perhaps the most intimidating step, but also the most important one, is to encourage believers to use their gifts outside the four walls of the church fellowship. The gifts are for the church's edification, but they can also be used in evangelism, healing, prophetic ministry, and the like.

Jesus used the gift of miracles to multiply fish and loaves for those just following Him around. Although at one point He accused them of only following Him because He fed them (see John 6:26), He miraculously fed them at least twice (see Matt. 14:13-21; 15:32-38). Why? To show the Father's love and bring folks to a place of decision—"do I want to be a disciple of Jesus the Messiah, or not?"

Likewise, believers using their giftings in public can also bring unbelievers to a place of decision. They may not all come to embrace our Savior, but they should not leave our presence untouched and unloved. The decision to follow Jesus is then up to them. But we can be catalysts of change in this world by using what God has supernaturally entrusted us with—His gifts and callings.

If leaders allow *"church-icus mice-icus"* to live and multiply like a virus and do not cure those who have contracted it or inoculate those who haven't, the members of those churches will never mature to become open portals for God's dynamically powerful love, which is what His Kingdom is all about.

About the Compiler

Frank DeCenso Jr. has been engaged in teaching the Bible and theological subjects since the mid-1980s. His venues have been churches, home groups, Bible studies, and online forums.

He is also the author of *Amazed by the Power of God, Presence Powered Living: Building a Life of Intimacy and Partnership with God.*

Frank and his wife of 16 years, Denise, attend Joy Vineyard Fellowship in Virginia Beach, Virginia.

About the Contributors

Dr. James W. Goll is the cofounder of Encounters Network, Director of Prayer Storm, and coordinator of Encounters Alliance, a coalition of leaders. He has shared Jesus in more than 40 nations worldwide. He has authored numerous books including *Prayer Storm, The Seer, Dream Language,* and *Angelic Encounters.* James and his wife, Michal Ann, who recently went to be with the Lord, have four children. He lives in Franklin, Tennessee.

Dr. Che Ahn and his wife, Sue, are the Senior Pastors of Harvest Rock Church in Pasadena, California. Che and Sue have four adult children, two of them married, Gabriel, Grace and Steve Baik, Joy and Kuoching Ngu, and Mary.

Che is also founder and president of Harvest International Ministry, a worldwide apostolic network of over 5000 churches in over 35 nations with the common vision of "Changing Lives, Transforming Cities, and Discipling Nations."

Che received his MDiv and DMin from Fuller Theological Seminary and has played a key role in many strategic local, national, and international outreaches, including being the President of TheCall from 2000-2004.

Che is author of numerous books including *Into the Fire, How to Pray for Healing, Spirit-Led Evangelism,* and *Close Encounters of the Divine Kind.* He travels extensively throughout the world, bringing apostolic insight with a Holy Spirit impartation of revival, healing, and evangelism.

Dr. Heidi Baker and her husband, Rolland, are the founders and directors of Iris Ministries. God has given them a heart for the poor, and they have been missionaries for the last 23 years in Asia, Europe, and Africa. For the past eight years, they have been ministering in the nation of Mozambique, where they are caring for orphans and street children while seeing a glorious revival in which thousands of churches have been planted.

Although Heidi holds a BA and MA from S.C.C., Vanguard University and a PhD in Systematic Theology from King's College, University of London, she learned more on the floor, under the weighty glory of Jesus for seven days and seven nights in Toronto, than in 10 years of university. Jesus told her, "You can do nothing without Me and nothing without the Body of Christ."

One third of Heidi's time is spent travelling throughout the nations preaching on passion for Jesus. Her heart is to impart His huge heart of love. Heidi loves Jesus more than life. Her life message is that all fruitfulness flows out of intimacy with Him (see John 14 and 15).

Jaeson Ma is president of Campus Church Networks, a ministry dedicated to fulfilling the Great Commandment and Great

Commission in this generation through catalyzing and cultivating church planting movements on every campus, every city, and every nation. He is a frequent speaker and strategic trainer for student revivals, training programs, outreach events, and conferences in the U.S. and worldwide. Jaeson prophetically speaks a radical message of passion for Jesus and compassion for the lost to the emerging generation.

He received three bachelor degrees in Bible Theology, Youth Ministry, and Business Management from William Jessup University. Jaeson also received a Certificate of Cross Cultural Campus Ministry from Fuller Theological Seminary.

He is an ordained pastor under the covering of Harvest International Ministries and has spoken at major events such as Global Day of Prayer and TheCall, and has been featured on the 700 Club. This last year, Jaeson released a book entitled, *The Blueprint: A Revolutionary Plan to Plant Missional Communities on Campus* as well as a worship rap album called *The Heart Back EP*. Currently, he resides in Pasadena, California, and loves to spend his free time reading, producing music/film, and spending time with friends and family, especially his mom.

Marc Dupont is the founder of Mantle of Praise Ministries, a ministry concerned with revival and restoring the prophetic edge to the whole Body of Christ. Marc ministers in two basic areas: speaking and impartation. Marc has served in various forms of church leadership for over 20 years, including teaching, preaching, counseling, evangelism, and church planting. Marc is an associate pastor with the Vineyard of Dayton. Marc, his wife Kim, their two daughters, and son reside in Dayton, Ohio.

Marc's books include: *The Elijah Years, The Church of the 3rd Millennium: Living in the Spirit and the Power of the Elijah Years, Toxic Churches, Pursuing Open Heavens,* and *Healing Today—When the Blind See the Lame Walk* (co-authored with Mark Stibbe).

Graham Cooke is a speaker and author who lives in Vacaville, California, where he is part of the leadership team at The Mission, formerly known as Vacaville Christian Life Centre. Graham has been involved in ministry since 1974 and is a popular conference speaker.

He also acts as a consultant to churches going through a period of transition to the next level of their corporate call. He is responsible for a series of training events involving intimacy, warfare, leadership development, and the internationally acclaimed School of Prophecy. Graham has written two books, *A Divine Confrontation...Birth Pangs of the New Church* and *Developing Your Prophetic Gifting.*

Steve Sjogren launched the Vineyard Community Church in Cincinnati, Ohio, in 1985 with 37 people. Under his leadership, the dynamic congregation grew to more than 6000 in average attendance. From the onset, VCC had a strong emphasis on servant evangelism, small groups, church planting, and caring for the needy. Following a medical accident in 1997, and during his recovery, Steve became the Launching Pastor.

Through the years, the church planting internship program and Steve's coaching efforts have produced several dozen successful church plants. Steve is currently focused on writing, speaking, and mentoring church planters. Steve's passion for evangelism, church planting, and leadership development is reflected in his writing. In 2007, Steve and his wife, Janie, began the launch of their fifth church planting adventure in the greater Tampa, Florida, area.

Dr. Craig von Buseck is a professional communicator and writer with a passion to touch the hearts of people with the life-changing message of the Gospel. For twenty years, Craig has impacted the lives of thousands of people as an author, speaker, musician, consultant, teacher, and Internet programming director. Craig von Buseck is Ministries Director for CBN.com. His passion is to share the truth of the Gospel through the mass media.

Wolfgang Simson has three passions in his life: the reformation of *ekklesia* back to biblical Kingdom standards, the return to Kingdom economics, and the unity of the smashingly attractive Bride of Christ. Wolfgang is of Jewish/Hungarian/German descent and is married to Mercy, who is from India. Together they have three sons, and they live in South Germany working "lobally" at a *local* Kingdom strategy that has *global* consequences. He is the author of 12 books that have been translated into 20 languages so far. His books include: *FridayFax, Houses That Change The World,* and *The Starfish Manifesto.*

Dr. Scott McDermott is Lead Pastor at Washington Crossing United Methodist Church in Washington Crossing, Pennsylvania. In addition to his leadership at the Crossing, Scott also teaches in the Doctor of Ministry Program at Perkins School of Theology, Southern Methodist University in Dallas, Texas. Scott holds a PhD in New Testament Studies from Drew University.

Kris Vallotton is the author of four books and an international conference speaker. He is the Senior Associate pastor at Bethel Church in Redding, California. He has been married to his beautiful wife Kathy for 32 years. They have four grown children and seven grandchildren.

Marguerite Evans is the National Coordinator for Soaking Prayer Centers USA (Catch the Fire Ministries), and she co-hosts with Gordon Robertson the Tuesday night CBN Spiritual Gifts Webcast. She is originally from South Africa. In 2000 she graduated from the Toronto Airport Christian Fellowship School of Ministry, Canada. She is also the owner of a finishing school for children, teens, and adults. Marguerite and her husband, Andrew, reside in Virginia Beach, Virginia.